STORYTELLING IN MIXED REALITY

Food For Thought in the Cinematic Metaverse

Clyde DeSouza

For Ethan Daniel Dsouza...as always

CONTENTS

PREFACE

The previous book, "Think in 3D" was 3 years in the making. This one took a lot less time...to compile into book form. It is however, the fruit of the past 9 years of work; an investment of time and spending of my own limited finances on hardware and software in a quest to learn this fascinating medium of immersive storytelling.

There are many how-to books on immersive filmmaking, and producing VR video. This is not one of them (though you might find a nugget or three in there!) I figured the topics chosen might appeal to the storyteller in us asking "what if" questions, as we map new territory...as we terraform the Metaverse with our unique contribution -that of the gift of story.

The result is a book, much like the previous one, that hopefully comes across as an interesting conversation between you and me...in bite sized chunks; easily digested, so we can seed new ideas as we delve into this emerging medium of "storyliving." I'm passionate about stereoscopy and Cinematic Virtual Reality and it will show on the pages that follow, where at times, I might even sound a bit...preachy? At those times...please feel free to drift off and make mental notes on your own ideas and thoughts on the topic(s) being discussed.

The last time we had a conversation about the book Think in 3D,

I'd suggested we do it while on a long haul flight. Might I suggest a good dining car on a nice train ride in Europe this time? The Linha do Douro in Portugal would be just great. We could even stop for a spot of wine tasting en route, but I'm open to any scenic train ride you might know of, where we can say cheers! and share food for thought on filmmaking in the Cinematic Metaverse.

PART 1 - MIXED REALITY STORYTELLING

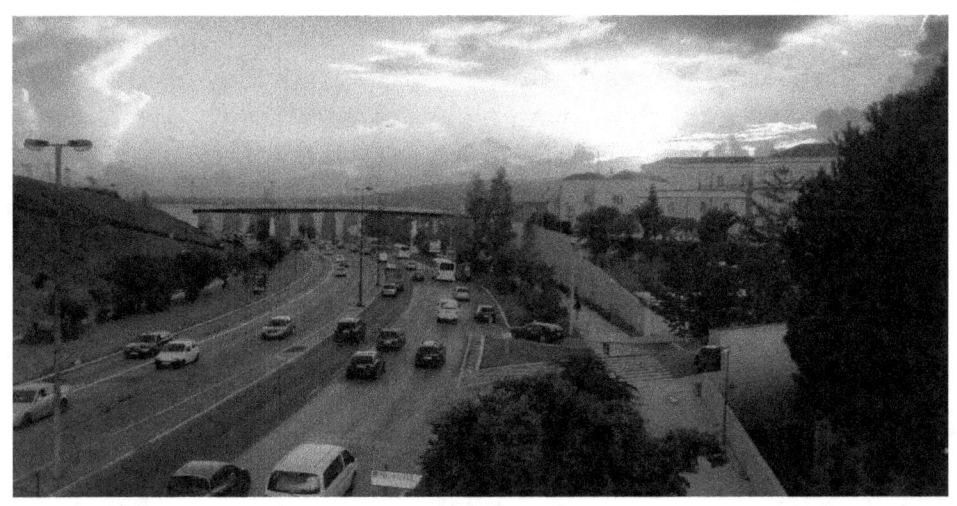

SAUDADE IN VIRTUAL REALITY

The Portuguese capture the finer nuances of "presence" beautifully, in a single word: "Saudade"

We've all experienced this feeling at some time. It might go something like this: It's evening and you're looking past your window, as the setting sun plays hide and seek with the clouds. The sky is overcast and a rumble of thunder, distant yet distinct, triggers neurons to fire in the recesses of your brain.

On your couch...alone, your hand reflexively caresses a cup of hot chocolate. The warmth of the cup and the aroma sends another trigger, activating memories that are slowly fading...Memories of how the two of you used to sit at home on days like these, the scent of your partners hair mingling with the scent of the wet earth outside, making you take a deep breath. Yet, they are not here now, and this might not even be the same window or the same couch...Déjà vu? The French come close, but no. Nostalgia? Not quite. Somehow *nostalgia* doesn't adequately describe this mix of yearning, and memories that are flooding you, while your mind, immersed in the scene, paints cinematic fragments of time and of a place that does not exist in your present real world.

Fragments Of Time In Virtual Reality:

What if there was a way of teleporting you? Of enabling one to re-live their saudade...on-demand? Total immersion and 'presence' is the holy grail every Director and Cinematographer strives for since the beginning of using moving pictures and sound in storytelling.

You reach out and wear a Virtual Reality headset.

Looking around, a smile forms on your lips. You're there! Your current couch and room might be different but the memories the two of you made from years ago trigger *saudades*. A thunderclap! overhead, thanks to spatial audio - and reflexes take over, making you grip the cup in your hand. Your fingers turn the VR headset's dial to mix in the real world. You squint as a shaft of sunlight catches your eye. A deep breath! -your senses adjust. You've just mixed your reality with one from a forgotten timeline.

In Dirrogate* the 2015 VR graphic novel, two of the main characters are in a long distance relationship. They use "Wizers" (visors with A.I) to rendezvous at different locations in the world. Haptics encode and transmit their touch - their "feel streams." While this would sound like science fiction just years ago, it's already becoming reality and will likely be the de-facto way LDRs (Long Distance Relationships) work for people separated by geography and time.

Dirrogate has a twist: One of the partners in the LDR is not in the real world anymore. While this perhaps borders on the taboo, it won't be science fiction for long. As we move into this new medium of storytelling, a few interesting questions come to mind:

• For people in LDRs - Army wives, the first inter-planetary settlers, or families living away from each other... could new "memories" be made in Virtual Reality?
• Would Virtual locations that loved ones log into, become "real" via stories told to each other in XR [extended / mixed reality]

Most importantly, would audiences experience "saudades"? Would it make them yearn to return to *your film's* story-world and timeline, more than their boring current real-world? Cinematic Virtual worlds need not be melancholy places. Saudades can be triggered even if storytellers extrapolate modern metropolises to what such cities would look like 25 years in the future. Filmmakers could aim to ask themselves these questions while embarking on each of their cinematic XR projects.

Meanwhile, if storytelling and movies evolve to such story-living experiences, the Portuguese just might have to re-invent the word, perhaps a befitting portmanteau; "Saud-ality"?

Dirrogate is a VR short film created in a Graphic Novel format. The VR experience might still be available for purchase in stereoscopic 360 at https://www.gum.co/dirrogate

IS CINEMATIC VR
REALLY VR?

virtual reality [vur-choo-*uhl* ree-al-i-tee] ◀) ☆

noun Digital Technology.
1. a realistic and immersive computer simulation of a three-dimensional environment,
   created using interactive software and hardware, and experienced or controlled by
   movement of the body. *Abbreviation*: VR

Above, is the by-the-book definition of Virtual Reality. Thus by default, VR is associated with a polygon rendered world, that gives the audience or participant, tools to interact with this computer generated world.

One camp of VR professionals believe this leaves no scope for mere 'spherical video' whether 4k or 8k or however 'realistic,' to be called VR, even if said video is a faithful recording and visual representation of the real world or one based on fantasy. It's still not VR to them even if displayed using the same display device that polygon based VR worlds use (HMD or Wraparound projection screen or C.A.V.E) After all -these professionals argue- for true VR, the viewer should be able to look around *and* behind objects in the VR world... People should be able to crouch and receive instant visual feedback of this translation in stance echoed back via a point of view change in the world.

In short, these professionals argue: Positional tracking = Virtual Reality —leading to that much desired state in VR: Presence. Now, the other camp will have none of this! and insist that spherical 360 video is also a Virtual representation of an environment (world) and can rightfully be called VR. Let's put forth arguments about what VR is and isn't, and then let both camps make up their minds.

But Carmack said...

Forget full 360 VR. Many people are quoting John Carmack, stating that if the God of VR has spoken...then 180 degrees (stereoscopic) video *is also* VR.

It certainly sounds that way when you first hear him in his talk at the Oculus Connect 2 event. But then when you listen closely, he says, "It's how you Frame video..." At this point he's getting to what matters...When does stereoscopic wideangle [180 degree] video transform into a VR experience? When it fits in and is part of the Virtual World being presented to the audience. When he speaks about building geometry (I call it CGI set extensions) around 180 degree stereo video, and the entire scene now seamlessly becomes one world...we've then successfully *suspended the feeling of disbelief,* and it gives audiences a sense of "presence." With that out of the way, let's back-track a little...

Is Spherical Or 360 Video, Vr?

To me, plain 2D spherical or 360 video leaves a lot lacking when it comes to suspending the feeling of disbelief. - ie. when watching 2d 360 video via an HMD, it's plain to see the scale of everything (except vista shots of say, the Grand Canyon or similar) is all wrong! People look 20 feet tall in the VR headset. Tables and chairs feel like skyscrapers. Unless...the intended VR world is meant to simulate the world in Gulliver's travels...don't do it!

It is indeed hard to call such presentations "Virtual Reality." This is perhaps where the former camp's main gripe stems from. When they say 360 video in not VR - there is a great chance they're referring to 2D 360 video. They have a valid point. But then again, they might not have experienced well-crafted and presented stereoscopic 180 or 360 stereoscopic 3D Cinematic visuals.

So...Is Cinematic Vr Really Vr?

The answer to me is a resounding YES...when presented well in Stereoscopic 180 or wrap-around 360, and when done right. Consider the following: VR is not just game worlds or CGI. How do you capture or create real life moments and memories and *re-live* them? Oh wait...Lightfield, Lidar and ToF volumetric 3D technology right? We'll certainly visit them when we can get 60 frames per second, 4k visuals out of those technologies.

Meanwhile, when the year is 2055 and we want to see what the Clinton Foundation did in Africa back in 2015, I for one will be happy and grateful to Felix and Paul Studios for creating a compelling VR "video" in 360 which allowed me to sit on a tattered green couch with two gentlemen a few feet away from an abandoned railway track looking down at the shanties...***immersed in that slice of history.***

Virtual 'Reality' —let the literal meaning of the phrase sink in for a moment...and not just the dictionary explanation.

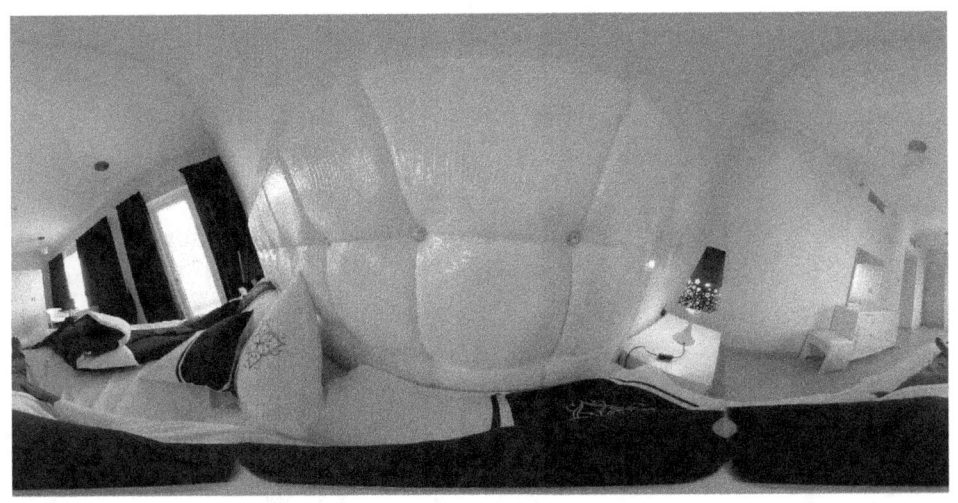

PRESENCE - IN VR FILMS

A few years ago there was an interesting discussion thread on Facebook's 360 filmmaker's forum. It was about the history of VR cinematography, (a compelling read), but it quickly came down to one point -the pros and cons of flat (2D) 360 degree video versus stereoscopic (3D) 360.

Comparing 2D 360 To S3d 360:

One of the arguments made in the discussion thread was that of audiences not caring whether a VR film was shot stereoscopically (S3D) in 360 or not. The claim being, that audiences are wowed sufficiently by VR itself, to not care what the medium of presentation was, but simply how spectacular the content was. As a disclaimer, I subscribe to the S3D 360 school of though. Without getting into lengthy back-story, I've reproduced below, my perspective (unavoidable bad puns will abound) on the subject. I believe the only way to make a fair comparison, and keeping narrative films in mind, is to show the same scene in 2D VR and then in 3D VR.

Here's one example taken from location scouting sessions during the creation of the 2015 Dirrogate VR graphic novel. Download it if you are reading the print version of this chapter, by typing the shortened Internet Archives address of the image [for as long as it remains hosted] https://tinyurl.com/2Dvs3D360 As unpolished as 360 images go, the image exhibits enough elements to discuss. There's also an S3D version below. Both images need to be seen in a VR headset.

Observations: When viewed in a VR headset:

• We notice the headboard is plastered to the wall.

• That is one huge Headboard, and those are some big *ss pillows.

• Am I (you) sleeping on a mattress on the floor, or is it a bed?

• Where does the bed end and the balcony door begin?

• The ceiling lamps that closer to the headboard - are they decals? or real lamps.

• How about the ceiling lamp pair further away? (Hint: Do their shadows lend depth cues)

• The angular cuts/shadows of the passage-way and the wardrobe —Do the shadows lend depth cues and thus offer the scene some sense of depth?

What I've learned from studying such scenes are:
I need to remove my socks when jumping into someone's bed...but

in all seriousness...If I were forced into making a *2D 360 movie*, a good DoP (director of Photography) would be indispensable. They would need to make sure depth and scale is being conveyed in VR either via lighting/shadows/contrast and/or, shallow focus etc.

Cinematography In Narrative 360Vr:

Download the S3D 360 image here: https://tinyurl.com/s3D360

Yes, there's some VR seams that kill the immersion but this is location scouting imagery from the year 2015 - well before VR editing software and off the shelf VR cameras were available, and, I own copyright on the images.

Observations:
   a) Suddenly we can start flirting with "presence."

   b) We also realize that my (your) legs don't really reach all the way to the passage / corridor entrance. We get a sense of scale because stereoscopic cues kick in.

   c) This, being a narrative scene, hopefully the acting & actress, who'll be part of the finished shot, will keep the audience's attention hooked to where the director wants —in the center of the room— long enough, that the only seams the audience notice, aren't on the walls.

I've shown many such scenes to people, and the results are as expected. It really is a night and day difference between 2D 360 Virtual Reality and S3D video VR. It's worth repeating that in conducting any fair test of audience appreciation of video based VR with headsets, comparisons have to be made using the same scene in 2D-360 and S3D-360. Many audiences don't know the difference, it's true, and that's only because they're being shown shoddy, flat video VR.

Further Observations:

• For Vista shots (Grand Canyon, Cityscape from atop the Eiffel tower, larger-than-life heritage architecture) ...2D 360 works and is spell binding.

• 2D 360 is degrees easier to stitch in VR video software, than s3d-360.

2D 360Vr V/S 3D 360 Vr:

1) Sense of scale -If one is aiming for "immersion" in VR video -you can't fudge 'presence' with giant people hovering around you. This will be evident when monoscopic (2D) captured video VR imagery is seen in a VR headset.

2) Most VR video that is not of grand vistas or aerial flight, pulls you (me) out of the scene and story.

3) I don't think a 2d-360 movie would do very well if shot from the conventional height of an actor. In VR you can't cheat scale, or depth. [Excuse me if I harp on this fact in multiple chapters]

4) A lot depends on the "angle" of objects and subjects in a scene and if they cast shadows - that's the only way to judge "distance" in 2D 360. Stereoscopic/Binocular spatial cues are non-existent. It's a wallpaper-wrapped-on-a-globe, world.

Motion parallax— introduces its own set of problems as 2D VR filmmakers come to depend on muti-cam 360 rigs built by Cinematographers or camera manufacturers who forget to [or sometimes can't] genlock sync cameras and may also exhibit jello-cam (rolling shutter) problems.

Even if these problems were fixed (via global shutter CMOS/CCD sensors and Machine vision cameras with genlock sync) the dependence on stitching multi-cam footage (with even moderate movement) is not error-free. This last point holds true for s3D 360 too, but citing motion parallax as an argument for entirely not shooting stereoscopic 180 or 360 VR in favor of shooting flat 2D "VR" still does not mitigate points 1,3 and 4, above.

Where I would certainly use 2D 360 is for aerial drone-cam coverage of events and visual documenting of larger than life structures. Where I'd recommend s3D-360 would be for virtual "telepresence" - teleporting the audience from a dusty battlefield to a bedroom as a narrative story unfolds.

If there's anything to be taken away from this essay, it is that, just as Palmer Freeman Luckey showed what a VR headset could be...so too should Cinematic VR storytellers strive to create experiences that lend as accurate as possible, a sense of presence to Cinematic VR storytelling.

With a focus on narrative S3d-360 storytelling, both factual and fiction based; to that end, I still feel the Director or Storyteller can be in control of a 360 "frame." Not having positional tracking, [so called 6DoF] does not, in my opinion, detract from the audience experiencing a good degree of *presence* in a properly scripted, and executed s3D-360 experience.

Headtracking (Pitch and ~~roll~~ yaw) for video based Virtual Reality is enough, because Spatial depth is a formidable "presence" cue, and when augmented with other monoscopic cues, makes for truly immersive visual storytelling.

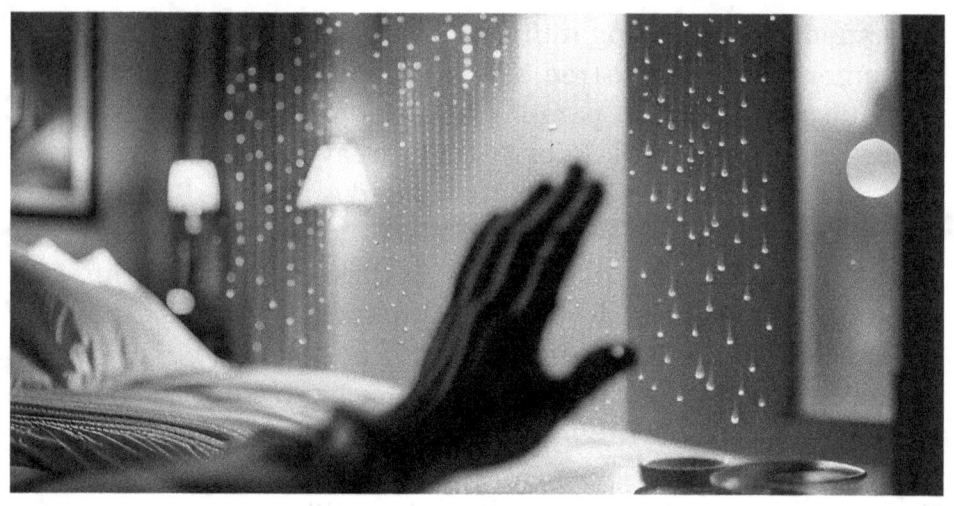

EMOTIONAL RECALL IN IMMERSIVE MOVIES

C an Virtual Reality imagery be a "trigger"? This line of thinking and proposition comes from method acting as used in Film and Theater, known as Affective memory and Emotional recall.

This is an acting technique of recalling the psychological or emotional response to a past event to evoke or invoke a stronger emotion during an actor's performance. Many times, jogging the mind to recollect moments and memories associated with a specific object, known as the "release object," is what triggers the desired emotional response called for by the Director during a performance; tears, for example.

Emotionally Enhanced Memories With Cinematic Vr:

For VR filmmakers, what is worth hypothesizing here is; could a subject, location or object, captured in stereoscopic video VR or volumetrically, *become* that "release object" for audiences watching a Cinematic VR movie? Could a scene in a VR movie with red balloons floating away or a close-up scene of candles being blown out at a child's party, trigger an emotional response in the audience remembering his/her childhood?

Or, could a scene such as a funeral and graveyard when viewed via a VR headset, affording the wearer a close-up view of a cement, granite or marble tombstone be the 'release' object that brings a flood of emotion in the viewer (if they have some repressed or forgotten memory of a family loss.)

The real world, captured stereoscopically and presented in a Virtual Reality setting, even if in low resolution, could have a larger emotional impact than a pure crisp CG recreation of the real world. It comes down to the feeling of Deja Vu. The brain shuttling through its memory bank -synapses firing- perhaps helping to re-construct long faded visual memories.

Some VR purists believe Virtual Reality should only allow for true interactive experiences, or at the very least, VR should let you "look around" objects. In the example cited above, it's worth considering that a viewer might simply be too emotionally rooted in the scene to want to "look behind" a tombstone. Such is the power and purpose of narrative Cinematic Storytelling in Virtual reality.

The movie Minority Report is one that managed to blur the line between science fiction and reality in many areas. In a memorable scene in the movie, we see what the possible effect could be, if someone today, was watching near holographic Virtual Reality home videos of loved ones in a VR headset with Digital See thru capability. These headsets can merge the virtual world with the real one. At the end of the clip, we see Tom Cruise looking out the window as rain pours and water drops trickle down the window pane.

For such a scene, the heavy rain could be thought of as the "trigger" for the actor (Cruise) while jogging his memory to recollect incidents he may have from moments in his real life, to bring a flood of emotions to enhance his performance.

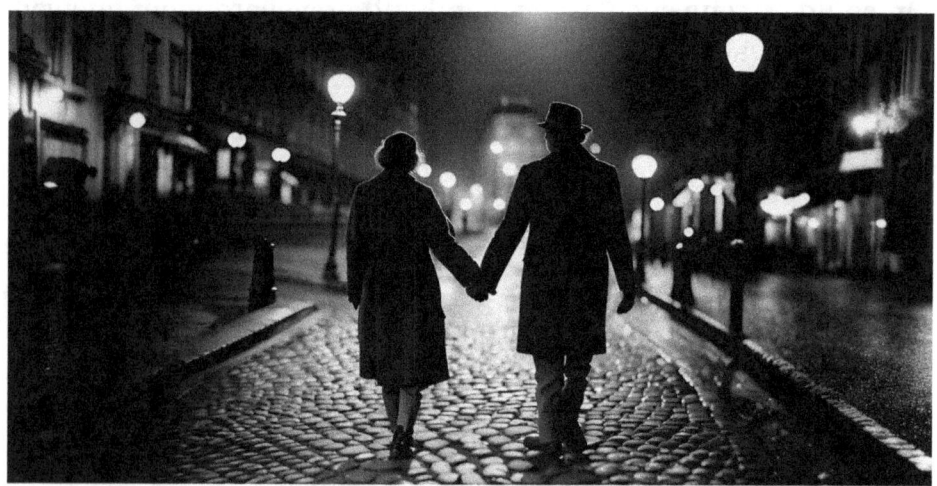

Immersive Vr: An Emotional Trigger For Audiences?

What's worth hypothesizing further is...Can an *entire* 3D created or captured VR scene be the "trigger" for audiences? In other words, can the feeling of "presence" -of being there- in Virtual Reality, trigger an emotional response in the viewer/audience that no 2D movie ever could? Could a person, a location, or entire scene, captured in 360 VR, and combined with positional surround sound, act as a trigger?

Maybe bringing back memories of happiness and a romance of

years ago, to members of the audience who may have strolled down a street in Paris...and maybe to others, memories of heartache, experienced on those very same streets?

The aim of movies is not always to re-create reality, but for the most part, Directors do want audiences to be immersed in the story unfolding, and if it has a profound personal effect on the audiences, that is what every storyteller strives for. Cinematic VR introduces a new medium for visual storytelling that was previously never available to Directors and Cinematographers.

Breaking The Fourth Wall In Vr:

"Did you think I'd forgotten you? Perhaps you hoped I had. Welcome back"

That's how Frank Underwood, a.k.a the actor Kevin Spacey, ends the first episode of Season 2 of the series, House of Cards. There's an actual sigh of relief from audiences when he looks directly at the cameras and utters those words. You see, F.U. has been talking to you (me) ever since Season 1 of the hit series, and we somewhat feel left out when the entire episode goes by, with him ignoring us. And this...is still a regular 2D TV show.

Imagine how devastating it would be, if this were a made-for-Netflix VR show. Yes, Netflix VR is a thing! We (I) would certainly take it personally if he sidelined us in VR as he does every so often, his trusted lieutenants. The language and the Grammar for Cinematic VR filmmaking is being written, every day. New storytellers are being born and contributing their unique vocabulary and 'voice' to the medium. While some veteran filmmakers might not yet be believers, the evolution of visual storytelling is already here.

There is an unparalleled connection between audience and story in VR when a storyteller knows how to manage the medium. An almost visceral reaction can be evoked in audiences when a Director knows how to leverage Virtual Reality to tell his/her story. We experienced the feeling first hand, in Oculus StoryStudios' "Henry" when he looks directly at us -in context- in the well-made VR film of the same name. Even though an animated movie, there is no denying the feeling of 'presence' the audience feels when viewing Henry on a VR "screen." While in traditional Cinema it's rare to break this fourth wall, in Cinematic VR - it begs you to!

This does not mean every VR [or XR] film should lead the audience *by-the-nose*, with an actor speaking to them. At least, the hope is that VR storytellers don't use it as a lazy way of keeping audience attention...the same way lazy Cinematographers do, with overuse of rack-focus and selective focus.

Omniscience In Cinematic Vr Filmmaking:

There is a need to respect and maintain the premise of "personal space in VR." For example, when shooting OTS (over the shoulder) scenes in VR films, as with Stereoscopic 3D movies, there's a need to maintain personal space. This fact won't be obvious in the many 2D VR videos being done by filmmakers.

In a 2D movie you can't really tell the spatial depth in a scene, but an OTS shot in stereoscopic 360 VR would look like the Objective Camera (or third person / audience) was actually resting their chin on the shoulder of the actor(!) if the camera was placed too close to the actor's shoulder. This would violate someone's personal space in real life (which is what our brains are being tricked into believing, a VR scene is)

Head Hopping In Vr Filmmaking:

In "Dirrogate," because the story is unfolding in Virtual Reality, it allowed me to experiment with a narrative point of view. Unless pointed out, no one who's seen the 10 minute VR experience has objected to the 'head-hopping' that is at play. What is of importance is, that in Virtual Reality, you get to allow the audience to 'gender-hop' seamlessly.

In conventional filmmaking, such head-hopping would be hard to pull off and would be jarring. How is it any different than a 1st person POV in a regular film? In a regular film you don't get to *look around* at will. This freedom when combined with spatial audio [the character's voice seems to emanate from within you] and the immersion of stereoscopic visuals, all trick the brain into believing *you are now part of the story!*

In Dirrogate, at 2:05 into the VR graphic novel film, a male viewer/audience gets to enter the head of Maya, access her (first person) point of view, while listening to her (female) voice - while now having a limited omniscient POV. It does not sound alien that your voice now has a different pitch and tone, whereas, earlier at 1:40 you certainly were accustomed to a man's voice as you 'became' Dan the main character, while you looked around at will, in the film.

Of course this can be attempted in conventional movie-making, but there is a difference, an important one...
In a VR film when head-hopping, you really do enter the new character's head. You can look around, independent of the Cinematographer's and the Director's wishes. This difference alone, and the fact that there is spatial depth & personal space, convinces the brain that you, the audience, *are there* in person.

In a Cinematic VR movie, you inhabit the character whose head you've hopped into!

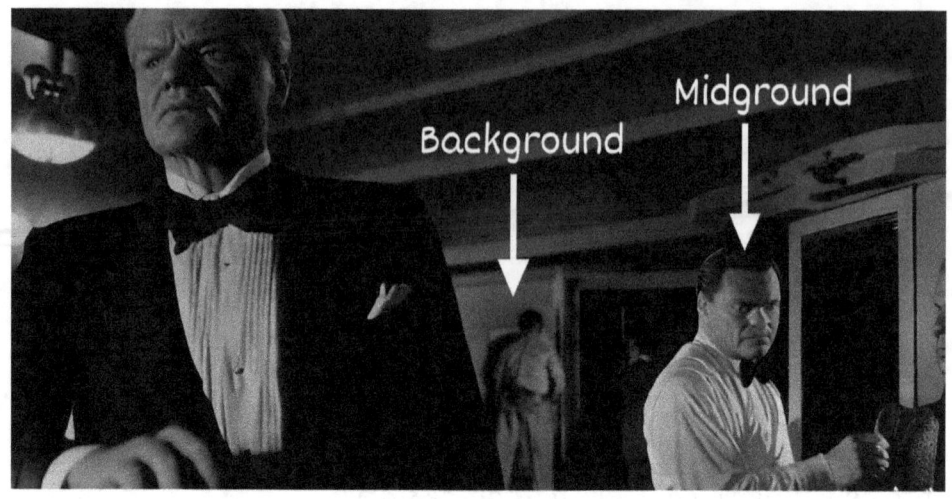

DEFINING A LANGUAGE
FOR CINEMATIC VR FILMS

C itizen Kane, back in the day, although a 2D film, has given enough clues to modern 3D film-makers on how to effectively use the medium of S3D...but no one really has the patience to listen. Lighting, Depth of field and yes – even hijacking the head-tracking stream [cut and reframe in VR] can work when creating movies on a 360 canvas.

When I started investigating this exciting medium, alarm bells would go off when I asked on the Oculus Rift / Game Engine forums about intercepting head-tracking and orientation info of those devices, but that's because so far it's only games that had been designed for VR. It's soon becoming evident that apart from the look-around voyeuristic possibilities offered by the medium, serious Directors and storytellers will look at retaining control of the "frame" if they are to be enticed into creating movies in Virtual Reality. So what would an immersive 360 Director's storytelling tool-box look like?

Lighting - With the temptation to look around a scene, a Director and VR DoP can use the age old technique of spot-lighting areas of importance to retain audience attention.

360 Positional Sound - Ambisonic, Binaural and Surround Sound authoring software are all now available to create scound-scapes that can aid in directing audience gaze.

Depth of Field - The pet peeve of Steresoscopic 3D film-making, unless done correctly. However, Bokeh is worth exploring in an immersive 360 environment, to guide audience attention. At least it won't be a lead-by-the-nose experience, as depth-of-field is sometimes abused by inexperienced DPs and Directors on 2D films, who rack-focus the audience to the point of nausea.

Limiting the Horizontal FoV - There is no rule per se that every scene should feature full wrap-around 360 views of the scene for the audience to explore. Recently, VR 180 movies are proving to be popular and easier to shoot (The entire crew and lights can be behind the camera's field of view.) The horizontal field of view can be restricted by the Director as a storytelling tool, for certain shots in a VR 360 movie. It's a creative call, and is what will contribute to the flavor of the overall VR experience.

Bokeh-ing the background

The concept of over use of Depth of field -a practice which I do not condone and label as lazy filmmaking; could actually be used to great effect if the background is completely Bokeh-ed out. i.e. there has to be no ambiguity for the eyes/brain to even attempt to fuse semi blur imagery, which would cause eye strain and headaches in both 3D movies, and especially more so in video based stereoscopic VR experiences.

Circle of Isolation:

In the book 3D A-to-Z: An Encyclopedic Dictionary, by Richard Kroon, available on Amazon, I'd contributed a definition for drawing audience attention, minus the eye-strain, in stereoscopic 3D filmmaking by coining the term "Circle of Isolation"

(Image Copyright: From the book: 3D A-to-Z: An Encyclopedic Dictionary)

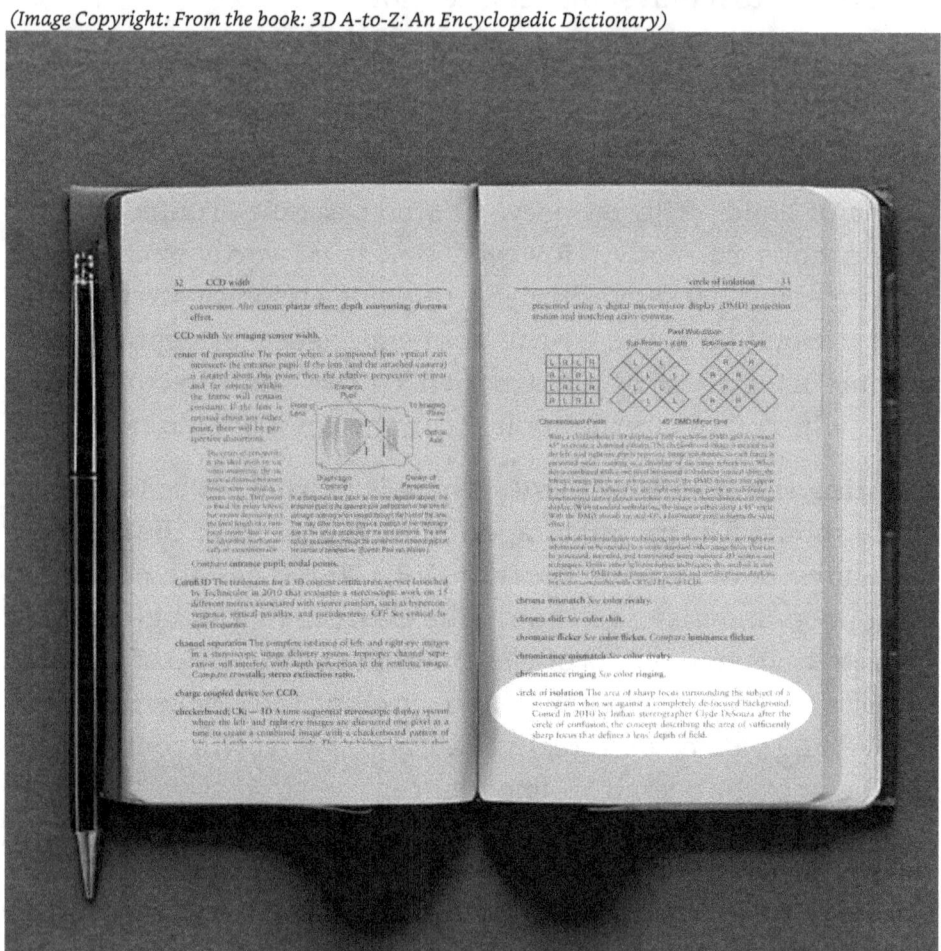

PART 2 - THINK IN EXTENDED REALITY

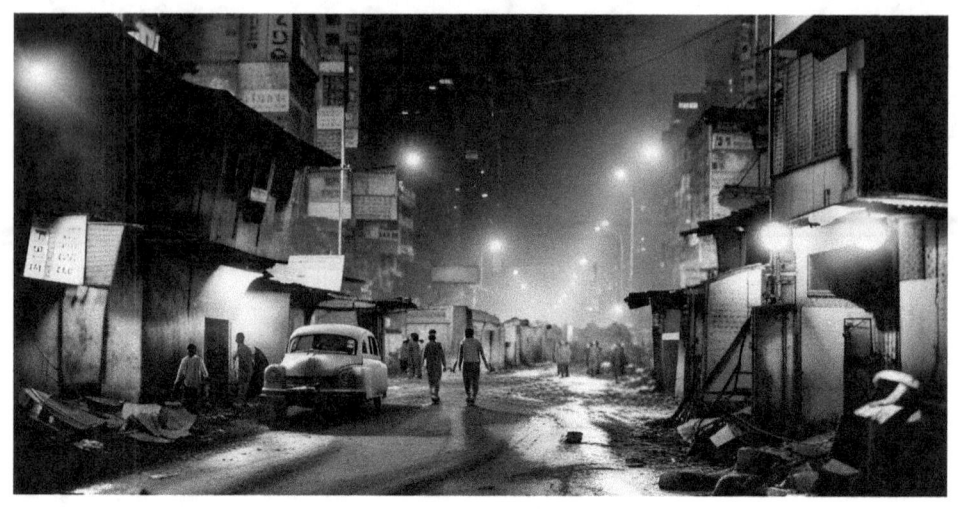

VR CINEMATOGRAPHY: MISE EN SCÈNE & CINÉMA VÉRITÉ

Stereoscopic 3D and Mise en Scene: Borrowing directly from Wikipedia, Mise-en-scène ("placing on stage") is an expression used to describe the design aspects of a theatre or film production, which essentially means "telling a story".

The term has evolved to represent a style of conveying information in a scene primarily through a single shot—often, accompanied by camera movement. It is in contrast to montage-style filmmaking, i.e. multiple angles pieced together through editing. So in essence, Mise-en-scene has been around for a long time, well entrenched in conventional movie making. What does Stereoscopic 3D then add to this style or technique of storytelling?

A scene when shot and presented in 3D, (via real or virtual stereoscopic cameras) provides spatial information of that scene. In 2D movie-making, without the ability to record this spatial information directly, Cinematographers have to rely on cues such as shadow, texture, movement of camera, framing, focus (and depth of field) to convey the 'depth' of a scene.

With the arrival of advanced and easily accessible High Definition Stereo 3D Cameras, VR Cameras and even Volumetric capture stages, a lot of what was taught in conventional movie-making has to be un-learnt, mostly because 2D techniques and styles of movie making, including framing and visual narratives... conflict with the sheer volume of "visual richness" that is present when spatial information in a scene is recorded.

Visual Grammar For 3D Cinematography:

The brain takes a while to "take in" a scene, and although still an optical illusion, contains such rich visual information, that if it were to be combined with for example, 2D cinematographic techniques such as fast cuts and pans, rack focus, or depth of field manipulation...it would lead to visual overload for the audiences, who may end up getting a headache as they struggle to make sense of all the visual stimuli being presented.

This I feel, is one of the premises, why Cinematic styles will change with storytelling in stereoscopic 3D VR. More information and visual narrative can be presented by exploring what is *within* the scene, and via *very* subtle camera movement rather than a montage like style made up of rapid cuts, frequently changing camera angles, or fast camera motion that is normally used to convey anticipation, excitement or other emotions in 2D movies.

Directors communicating with Immersographers on their next Cinematic VR film or Factual story epic, can learn a few technical 3D catch words and concepts such as Floating Windows,

Convergence, Divergence and H.I.T. which are explained in the book, Think in 3D, available on Amazon.

Remember: A pristine Cinema and Theatrical screen ready 3D movie can be extracted from a 180 or 360 VR film.

Mise En Scene + 3D = Boring Action Movies?

If a new visual grammar is to be developed for 3D Storytelling, would this then lead to boring action movies that present an almost "Locked down Camera" POV (point of view) on a scene? Not necessarily. The premise of this discussion is to use Mise en Scene in a Cinema Verite style, and to use it creatively to present a story. There's no reason not to use multiple "view ports" or camera framing to present a battle scene in 3D. The technique would be to not cause audience dis-orientation that may occur by a follow-the-action technique as used in a 2D filming style.

On a 35 foot wide or larger screen (Imax®?) the establishing shot of a Battle-field captured by a stereo 3D camera at eye level, and presented via high brightness Digital Projectors, has an effect of converting the Cinema screen into a window onto a virtual battle-field, with the audiences sitting as spectators in an arena like setting. The texture of the sandy terrain and dust could almost be tasted by the senses, if, the audience is given enough time for their brains to *digest* the environment. To put this thought into perspective: In the 3D movie trend-setter, Avatar...How many people can really remember the detailing on the foliage, or the exquisitely created surroundings *during the battle scenes or chases in the movie?* But, Cinema screen immersion is sooo...2010's

VR headsets are like Imax® screens strapped to audience's faces!

Directors have less control with Stereo 3D?

Mise-en-Scene would mean extra preparation and choreography of action and movement on the set, with less cheating than is possible with 2D "filming" styles. This is a tradeoff that should be expected, and should not be seen as a shortcoming but as an opportunity to "immerse" the audiences into the story.

With the ability of the audiences to visually wander around the rich vista unfolding around them, will this make the Director feel he/she has a less important role as the story teller? It does not have to be that way. Stereo 3D presents the Director with the opportunity to truly suspend the feeling of disbelief...the very holy grail of moving picture storytelling.

Mise En Scene And Cinema Verite In 3D Vr:

Borrowed from Parlez-Vous.com: Cinema verite is part of the broader artistic tradition of realism and the cinematic tradition of documentary film making. These realistic traditions are aimed at showing man's real situation in life rather than at providing him with an escapist fantasy experience which an audience will enjoy watching and will pay for by coming out to the movies in very large numbers. So, it's a little like Documentary film making, but not exactly. To make it easier to understand and further referencing Wikipedia,

> *"Pierre Perrault sets situations up, and then films it, for example in Pour la suite du monde where he asked old people to fish for whale. The result is not a documentary about whale fishing; it is about memory and lineage. In this sense cinéma vérité is concerned with anthropological cinema, and with the social and political implications of what is captured on film."*

Some popular movies that demonstrate a Cinema Verite technique (if not the spirit) are: The BlairWitch Project, Cloverfield, District 9. TV shows include NYPD blues, Lost, and The Office.

The movie SlumDog Millionaire; had it been shot in stereoscopic 3D, would have been a poster movie for a 3D Cinema Verite movement. It had everything from good use of Mise en scene, to cinema verite style handheld high resolution camera capture of urban reality. The pace and framing of the movie would have had to be changed no doubt for 3D, but under the guidance of a good stereographer, every scene could have been a cinematographic stereo masterpiece, re- defining the medium of story telling through moving images.

Rather than resorting to gimmick like usage of 2D movie conversion to 3D, which has a place as a VFX technology to correct for errors such as un-wanted lens flares etc., Directors and Cinematographers should experiment and investigate storytelling techniques now that filmmaking with true immersion is possible.

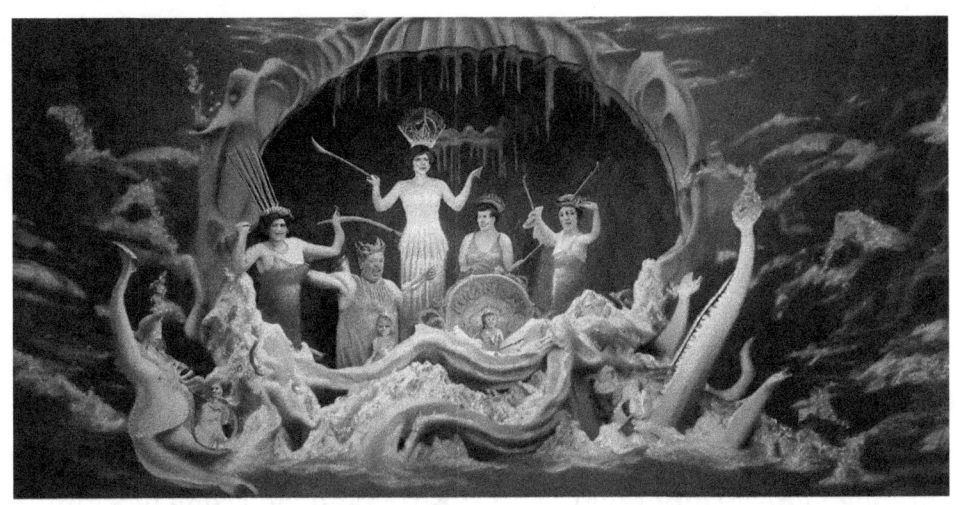

HUGO: DEEP STAGING AND KEYFRAMING IN 3D

Hugo, the movie, is a case study in how stereoscopic 3D can and should be used as a new medium of visual storytelling. I remember being excited to finally get a chance to see the movie a few weeks later than its release date, having read many rave reviews.

Key Framing V/S Montage Cinematography In 3D

What was good about Hugo in 3D? Undoubtedly it had to be the lovely long key-framing camera work in many scenes. Whether by accident or actual planning, CGI wizardry, motivated edits and cuts, and/or other means...This was one visually well done masterpiece of Stereoscopic 3D Cinematography.

In typical film making it is easier to establish geography of a scene, or tell a story by assembling different shots of the same scene recorded by different camera positions and from different angles. On the other hand however, it would need much planning and scene blocking to do "keyframed" style camera movement.

As a simple example, if the scene is of a person walking into a room and moving into position in-between two other people in the room, it is much easier to shoot this scene by placing the camera at different locations around the room to capture the intended effect (montage), than it is to: plan, do scene blocking, lay track and then dolly the camera along with the person, swinging the camera around at the right moment so as to frame the actor as he gets into final end position.

3D Shot Planning:
It takes planning, rehearsal and skill, and we are still talking 2D movie scene! In 3D it's a whole different ball game of Previz, correct camera interaxial, looking out for stereo window violations, and yet keeping the camera work fluid and the scene itself interesting. This is the reason audiences were paying the extra dollar! (similar to a gourmet meal v/s fast food)

This is what was done right in much of Hugo, and in beautiful well-crafted 3D. Granted today's attempt at keyframed camera work is rarely what long takes were, back in the day when Hitchcock tried it out. But even he used the cleverly choreographed "10 minute" Long take. In today's film making, the use of CGI camera flight paths, motion control camera rigs and other tricks are allowed. As long as the end result is good camera dwell time, and an audience immersing Stereoscopic 3D experience.

"In Hugo, even the Card Boarding was Motivated"

There is much talk amongst stereographers and 3D cinematographers on the subject of long lenses (zoom lenses) and the "cardboarding" effect it creates in 3D movies. Why is this *also* relevant to VR films? Well, the rapid proliferation of VR 180 films in on us. While it's true they are mostly shot with fish-eye lenses giving a 180 - 200 degree field of view - there's no reason scenes can't be shot with telephoto lenses where the story calls for such (view through binoculars, keyhole, security camera view, etc.)

Getting back...In layman's terms, cardboarding is noticeable when one shoots a scene with a telephoto or zoom lens. What happens is, longer lenses "compress" depth, so in 3D, the scene will look like several layers of cardboard cut-outs arranged in 3D space. The same effect is visible when watching the world via a pair of binoculars. Did Hugo have Cardboarding? Yes, but even that was "motivated" I said to myself, in the Diorama scenes! In the non-diorama scenes, there may have been a few shots where cardboarding was visible, but I would need to see the movie again to confirm, as were some possibly 2D to 3D converted shots I remember, in the Library scene.

A well-made 3D Film:
To round of this 3D Critique of Hugo, here are a few more observations:

1) **Motivated Camera Placement and Editing:**
Throughout the movie I noticed a careful balance of camera movement and timed cutting (edit) of a shot, so as not to give audiences any feeling of miniaturization (hyper stereo)

2) **Use of Depth Budget and Negative Z-space:** Hugo did not shy away from pulling characters right to the edge of the stereo window, and although I thought that some scenes with the Inspector General or Ben Kingsley were too in-your face for comfort, because the eyes were "converging" (going cross-eyed) rather than diverging, (going wall eyed) it worked.

3) **3D movies with meaning**: I liked the bit on preserving film history, and although it was a mini-documentary, the lesson was well taught to younger audiences. Years ago, I'd written an article on how Hollywood could preserve and document real world architecture with 3D movies...Hugo made a related point. Just as the Digital Assets of "Pandora" from the movie, Avatar, could make for a real-time Climate Change lesson for kids, similarly, the *preservation-of-old-films* message could make for an interesting 3D VR mini-documentary. This shows how an immersive VR movie can cross-over to the education sector where attention spans are short, and immersive 3D VR content can help bridge that gap.

Verdict: The movie set the bar a couple of notches higher for stereoscopic 3D filmmaking and is a must watch for any Director, Immersographer or Immersive Storyteller.

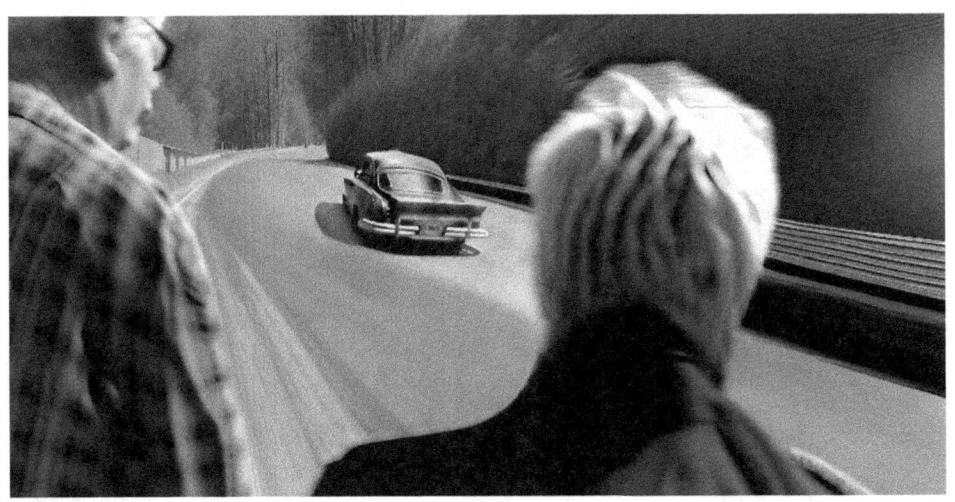

VR FILMMAKING AND MOTIVATED CAMERA MOVES.

When Directors and Cinematographers start responding to the call for immersive VR movies by the "big three" VR Headset and eco-system makers, one important aspect could get overlooked.

Decades of 2D movie making experience of creating depth in a scene via lighting, lens effects, and framing, will need to be un-learnt. In 2D it's easy to "cheat" depth. (I told you, I'd be repeating it ad-nauseam in the book!) In 3D look-around filmmaking, one does not need a montage of different angles (cuts) to represent the geography and spatiality of an environment in VR, as is needed in a 2D movie. The one thing that 3D excels at, is in faithfully reproducing spatial depth in a scene.

Crafting a VR depthscape:

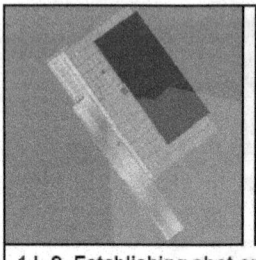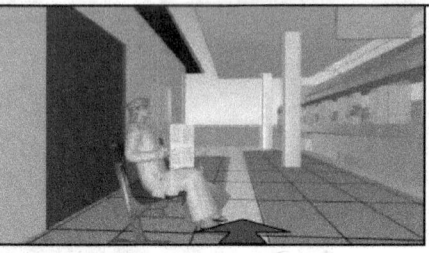

1 L.S. Establishing shot opening of movie
MOHAMMED, a man in his 40's is sitting on a bench reading a newspaper. No one is seated beside him. Beside him there is a bottle of water and a bag of chips.

Camera Height: 2.91m | Focal Length: 6.4mm | Angle of View: 74°
Roll: 0° | Tilt: 0.0° | HIT: 20pixels | Interaxial: 30mm | Screen Plane Dist: 1.92m | Dist to Max Offset: 3.07m

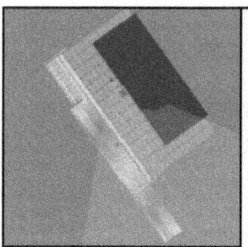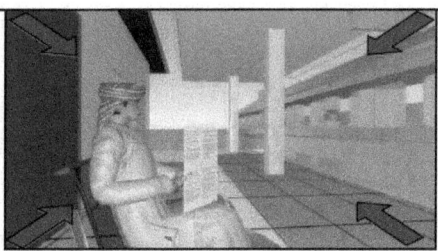

2 M.C.U. Mohammed looks left to check Metro
He turns to his left
and checks to see if the metro that's arriving is his.

Generated with FrameForge 3D
(Stereoscopic 3D version)

www.realvision.ae/blog

Camera Height: 2.91m | Focal Length: 6mm | Angle of View: 77°
Roll: 0° | Tilt: 0.0° | HIT: 20pixels | Interaxial: 20mm | Screen Plane Dist: 1.20m | Dist to Max Offset: 1.92m

Look at the image in this chapter; the man sitting on the bench. It's a previz story board done in the excellent software FrameForge. Of interest to us is the Camera data at the bottom of each panel. It shows Camera height at 2.91 meters from the ground. In a Virtual Reality film, think of this number as the "neck" height the VR Camera is placed at in the Virtual world. It's also the height that we'll thus give our audience (who feel there really *are inside* that world)

What is the Motivation for placing your VR Camera at 2.91 meters?

This is the first question an "Immersographer" has to ask a Director or Cinematographer, while they frame a VR scene. It may well be that the shot is not married to the script, except to show an establishing shot of a train station with a man on a bench reading a newspaper. In that case, it's OK to place the camera at such an arbitrary height. However, what if the movie is meant to "afford presence" -one of the buzz phrases in Cinematic VR filmmaking- and the script reads:

"The detective approaches a man sitting on a bench reading a document, and comes closer to have a glance at what he's reading".

We should be aware that in 3D VR, the spatial dimensions of a scene are faithfully recorded and presented, so the VR camera placement at 2.9m above ground would yield a POV of the detective running a risk of seeming like the detective is a 3 meter tall man! Things get more complicated if in an effort to preserve "stereo roundness" or for other reasons, the interaxial (Stereo 3D camera base, or lens spacing of the VR camera) leads to hyper stereo and thus "miniaturizes" the seated man. In a regular film, this is not a concern as depth and perspective are cheated. In Stereo 3D, a film maker has to step back, take a macro look at the scene and then decide on what the motivation is for a particular choice of camera placement. In a 360 Virtual Reality scene, where the audience has freedom to look around the scene, *Gigantism* (the VR headset wearer feels like a giant) might pull the wearer out of their suspension of disbelief mode.

Challenges in Designing an S3D VR Camera Rig:
Careful orchestration of a VR Camera move (correct interaxial,

timed cut, taking the proper amount of dwell time into consideration) will lead to compelling Virtual Reality Cinematography in scenes involving Jibs and Crane shots. Of course, in simple Mise-en-scene VR cinematography, it gets easier as there are less variables to look into. It's easiest when creating a VR movie completely in CG or via a Realtime Game Engine.

Things get very interesting and challenging for live action, look-around 360 VR cinematography. First time VR filmmakers will eventually discover how to use HIT (Horizontal Image Translation) to balance depth volume of a VR 180 movie or 3D 360 VR scene. Currently there might be only a handful of astute Cinematic VR filmmakers who know how. But even then, it's for depth sweetening of the entire 3D volume in the scene. HIT is addressed in the earlier book; Think in 3D.

Examples of Camera Motivation:
If an actor in a scene is riding an elevator going up, or a Helicopter lifts off from a helipad with an actor looking down, this would be motivation for where the camera is placed in S3D Virtual Reality. Ultimately the premise of Motivated Camera movement is the choice of the Director or DoP. They have to have the ability to think in VR!
To see how Crane and Jib shots could break the suspension of disbelief and pull audiences "out" of their state of immersion (in regular 3D movies) pay close attention to these scenes from 3D movies such as:

1) Transformers: When the main actor comes out of his parents mobile-home.

2) Drive Angry 3D: A high shot looking down on a gun fight in the motel room. Side note: in S3D, bigger is better. So a cinema sized screen does save this scene to a certain extent from extreme miniaturization. A different choice of interaxial (lesser) and lens, would have made for a better 3D scene, yet if this scene was shot

in 3D VR, the audience would feel like a giant spectator watching a diorama unfolding in front of them.

This discussion is not a set of rules, but more a guide, aimed at seeding ideas as we move forward toward defining a new language and grammar in Virtual Reality Filmmaking.

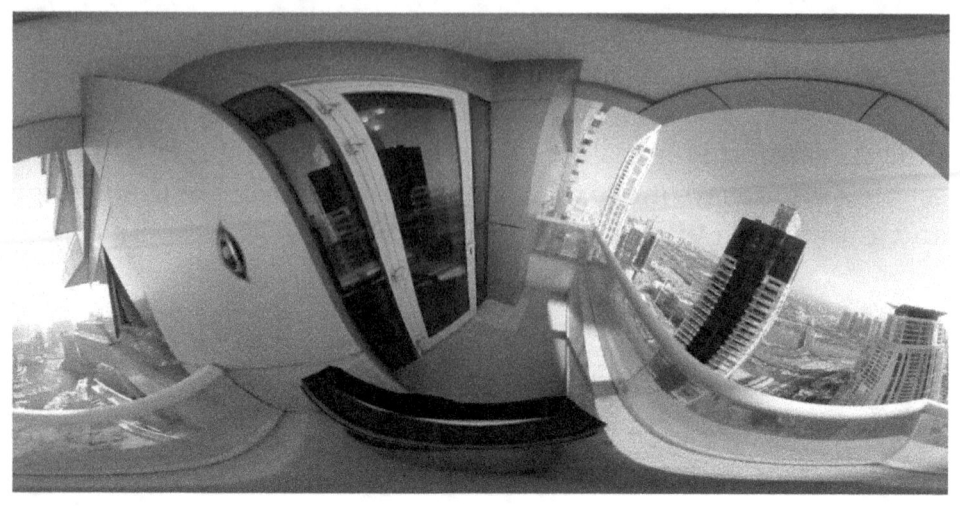

CAMERA BLOCKING IN CINEMATIC VR MOVIES

T ake a look at the header image. Chances are, most VR professionals will cringe and chastise you for not "leveling" the horizon.

One can't blame them. They are professionals who have been producing panoramic images for the past couple of decades (if not more) and meticulously leveling the camera during principal photography, or massaging the image pairs through stitching software while correcting for anomalies to produce aesthetically pleasing finished panoramic images. Once those images were polished, they were usually printed in large format posters, center spreads, planetarium domes and sometimes even displayed electronically on websites with click and drag interactivity, allowing for the audience to pan around the view.

Then...HMD's came along. This gave birth to "Cinematic VR" - or, where panoramas weren't stills anymore, but captured as moving images with dedicated multi-camera rigs. Overnight "VR Cinema" studios cropped up, with varying levels of expertise.

However, since the art of visual storytelling in Cinematic VR is still in it's infancy, let's take a look at a few things possible when you capture the entire 360 field of view. There are pros and cons when looking at what's possible when manipulating 360 frame as a storytelling tool. Re-framing is one such possibility. More on that in a few seconds. Today there are -and to use that oft misused term- literally, a couple of studios worthy of mention in the domain of stereoscopic 3d 360 VR Storytelling.

Let's look at an example of how a Cinematic VR scene captured from a single vantage point in 360, can be re-synthesized to produce different viewpoints.

FADE IN:

EXT. DAN'S BALCONY - DAY

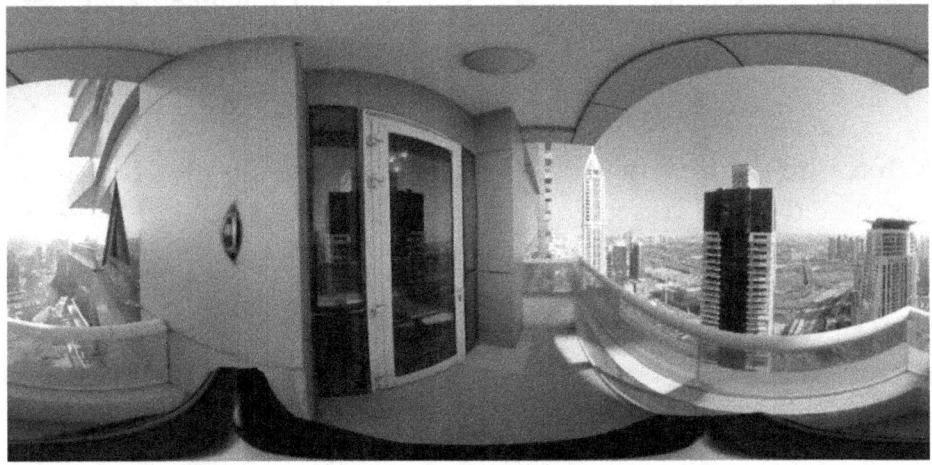

Dan sits on a bar-stool, smoking a cigarette taking in the view. The rich life. We hear him exhale.

EXT. DAN'S BALCONY (LATER) - DAY

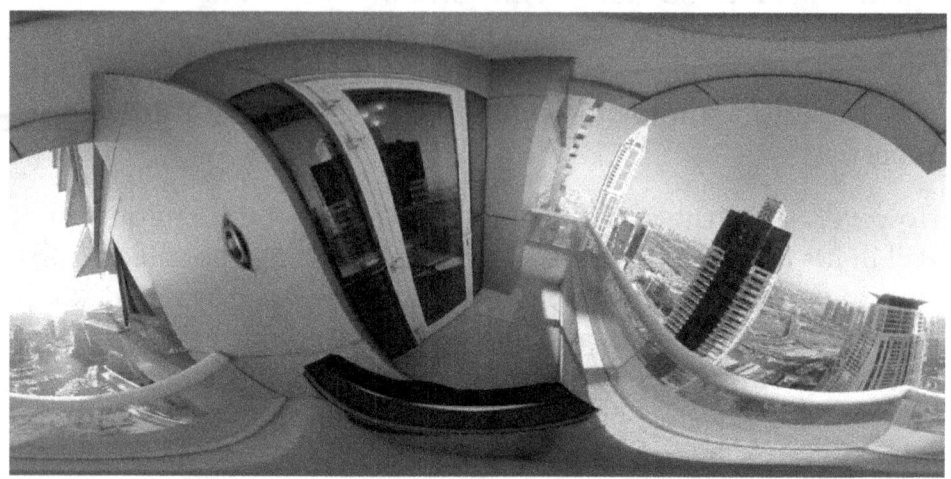

Dan has climbed the bar-stool; looking at the spent cigarette butt in the corner of the balcony...He turns around, the lag in his visual cortex and the blurry resolution in his field of view almost making him lose balance. Life's not worth living in a one dimensional flat world. It has to be 3DVR or nothing. Dan notices the embedded fish eye in the wall, staring back at him... There was hope...The fisheye was a clue that his world was not one dimensional after all.

FADE TO BLACK...

What's interesting here is that the shot is a single panorama (extracted from a stereo pair) and different camera angles are synthesized from the same shot, **after-the-fact**, allowing a Director to "own the frame" i.e: set the stage for a new narrative shot/scene, *before* letting audiences take over.

Remember, in a VR movie, control changes hands the moment the audience wears the headset. They're now the Director and Cinematographer to a certain extent.

Re-Synthesizing - Camera Blocking In Vr 360:

Re-synthesizing of a view-point in a 360 scene can be done in conventional 'stitching software.' Do you as an Immersive Storyteller or Director or Cinematographer need to know how stitching software works? Not really. Editors might need to know, but it helps if you have an overview of the different processes that go into creating an immersive experience.

For the indie VR filmmaker, Adobe's After-effects with its slew of image manipulating features can also be used to change direction (compass direction) of where the camera is facing at the start of a new scene or shot, including setting of view-point tilt among other parameters. Of course, such a view point can be captured during principal photography, but it's nice to know it's also achievable after-the-fact. One thing that needs to be remembered is, if the scene is captured in stereoscopic 360, scale and depth will be baked in, and you can't then cheat these aspects so easily.

Just as filmmakers had to re-learn a lot of how a "frame" (proscenium?) could be manipulated for effect in conventional 3D movies, so too must Immersographers and Directors. They must learn to 'think in VR' much the same as 3D filmmakers learned to "Think in 3D"

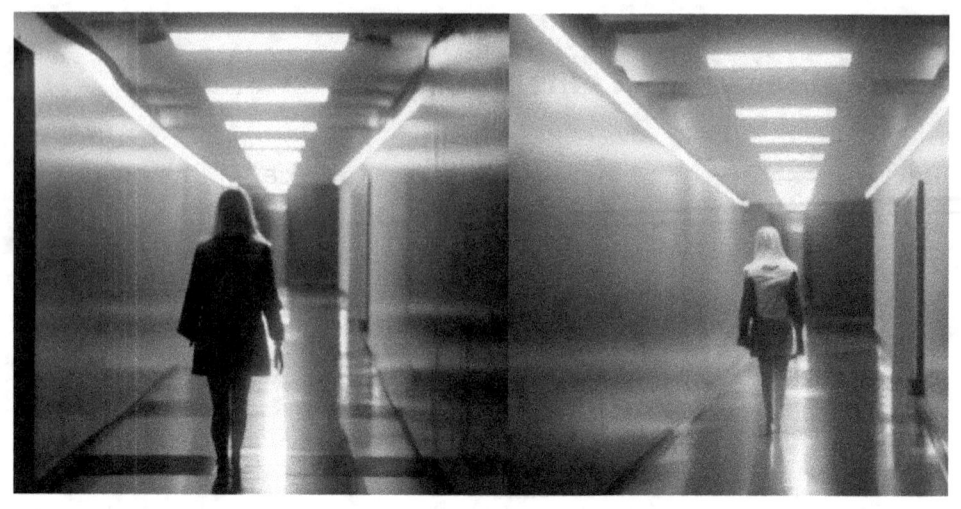

DEPTH CONTINUITY IN NARRATIVE VR FILMS.

I n 2016, as Cinematic VR video picked up steam, Adobe showed off "CLOVER VR" a kind of Premier Pro for editing VR video, in VR. The concept and the need is very cool and much needed.

While watching the demonstrator showing a cut, I immediately thought of an older essay I'd written (adapted below) on depth continuity and how it's as relevant to video based Virtual Reality as it is to cinema 3D films. If the demo of the CLOVER VR were to have shown stereoscopic VR scene cutting, then editors working with a VR headset would quickly experience, first hand, the importance of depth continuity, particularly, in a narrative VR film.

Stereoscopic 3D Depth Continuity:

In traditional 2D films the task of maintaining continuity from scene to scene is that of the Script Supervisor (and Director). The same goes for "depth" in a 3D or VR film. For instance, in a 3D movie, if a scene features a person walking down a corridor into the distance, the next camera angle should'nt show the person to have traveled half way down that corridor in a matter of a couple of seconds. Unless, this is done intentionally as part of an effect of speeding up time.

It's even more jarring if (and I don't recommend the practice) the scene calls for a gimbal assisted follow of the actor, and the editor abruptly decides to cut to save screen time. Remember: The audience wearing the headset can decide they are the "cameraman" walking behind the actor, in a Cinematic VR film. They'd be in for an uneasy time if there was a sudden depth-jump by a cut.

The 'Spatiality' of a scene:

In regular 2D movies, we cheat...a lot! That's one of the ways those stunts involving a person crossing a railroad track at seemingly the very last second while a train approaches, works. The use of long lenses compresses depth and makes it look like the train is a lot closer than it actually is. In Stereoscopic 3D and Stereoscopic 360 or "VR video films", this cheating of depth is very near impossible to do. The one thing that stereoscopic 3D gives us, is the ability to record and present "Spatial information" or unlock the depth channel in a scene.

S3D Depth Continuity is more than just Cut matching:

Take a look at the two images at the start of the chapter. If it was a scene shot with stereoscopy best practices, then the 'immersographer' along with the Cinematographer, Director and Editor (it's crucial to have the Editor on-board) would need to ensure both the shots "match" in depth continuity. The actual "deepness" of the corridor needs to match in both shots if shown at two different times during the movie.

One way to ensure this, is to shoot all scenes involving a particular set, at the same time, so camera interaxial and placement are set. This gets important in VR 180 films as well as 360 VR films. What an immersive storyteller and filmmaker needs to remember is, that during post production (stitch / edit) phase of a film, someone could change the perceived 'depth' of a scene. There are other things to take note of to maintain depth continuity:

1) Ensuring the lens settings are the same (in a stereoscopic movie.) In a VR movie, lenses are usually fixed fish eyes, yet as Cinematographers know; lenses 'breathe' and not in unison! These can lead to optical anomalies showing between the left and right eye images captured.

2) The Interaxial distance of the lenses on a VR180 or 360 camera, or toe-in (convergence) if any, is noted and re-applied when shooting at the same location. - For a 360 VR movie, it would not be kosher to set interaxial, on set... (it could be done, but that's beyond the scope of this chapter)..so for VR it is usually limited to camera placement, when executing a hard cut.

3) **Temporal Depth Continuity:** The time taken to travel a distance needs to be approximately the same, depending on if the character or camera is previously shown as running or walking. Another example of a depth mismatch is in cuts. In some 3D movies in the past, there were scenes where camera placement and lensing wasn't 'marked' with depth settings. This led to bad practices of cutting to a solo shot of one of the actors speaking, and then to a wider shot (where either the camera is moved or lens focus changed) leading to a completely different depth which is very noticeable.

In a VR headset, such Cinematic VR content leads to eye-ball gymnastics in audiences. The stress and strain is on a subconscious level, but is one of the reasons people remove VR headsets, close their eyes and massage their eyebrows with their thumbs and index fingers.

VR Depth Continuity - The Script Supervisor's Job?

That question is open to debate at this stage of VR movie making. As time goes by and more experience is gained, it's natural that the DP would want to take charge of the entire composition of the VR "frame." The word frame is in quotes because today in VR filmmaking, a lot of established terminology from regular filmmaking, is open to new interpretation.

Getting back...should the script supervisor be in-charge of the depth script as well as the movie script? Or, should the depth-script be in the hands of the Cinematographer, and can they pay attention to maintaining depth continuity in addition to their other tasks.

As VR movie making evolves, one debate that will soon be over is whether there's a need for an Immersographer. I would argue yes, there is a need. For the very same reason there is a need for a Best Boy and Gaffer. An Immersographer is certainly recommended for this one reason alone: taking care of depth continuity during a shoot while consulting with the Director and Cinematographer, and in post, with the Editor.

Can these jobs be offloaded to the script supervisor or DoP? Yes, in indie productions one person fills many boots, but in a well-planned (and financed) VR film, Depth Continuity could be better handled by someone well versed in the art of immersive storytelling.

Motivated Camera Placement and Depth Continuity:

In the reimagined image below, inspired by the 3D movie Drive Angry, the intent is to show another kind of Depth Continuity mismatch: Perspective mismatch. The creative framing of the scene shows a between-the-shoulders objective framing. In a normal 2D movie (not a 2D 360 movie) this framing would look just fine, suggesting the car is further away and thus smaller in size. Can you guess why this won't work in a 2d 360 movie? Because, when viewed in a headset, those heads and shoulders would tower above you! (there's no stereoscopic 3D depth cues)

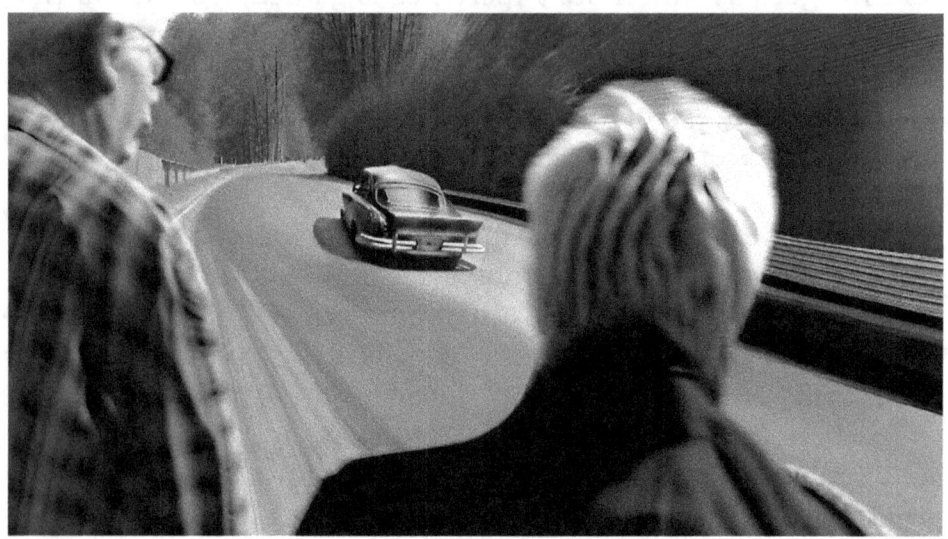

When wearing a headset, you are 'in' the movie world! The scene would look perspectively wrong in flat 2D 360 VR. The scale won't add up. The wearer of the headset feels 'shorter' and the scene looks like the two characters are perched on higher ground looking down at the car. Yet in the very next cut (in the movie Drive Angry 3D), we get the POV of the driver of the car looking at a roadblock with the two previous characters now shown standing on solid ground.

If this were a 3D VR movie, Depth continuity would not match, because in 3D 360 (let's call it Cinematic VR) the terrain -the ground, is quite easily accessed by the audience, simply by them looking down, with the VR headset on, towards their feet.

In VR movie editing, the editor now has to learn a couple more aspects of shot and scene continuity; that of camera motivation, perspective, and depth matching between cuts. An Immersographer with experience and depth intuition would keep a lookout and red-flag such events during principal photography or at least during edits if he/she is present during post production of a Cinematic VR movie.

DEPTH RAMPING: IN VR

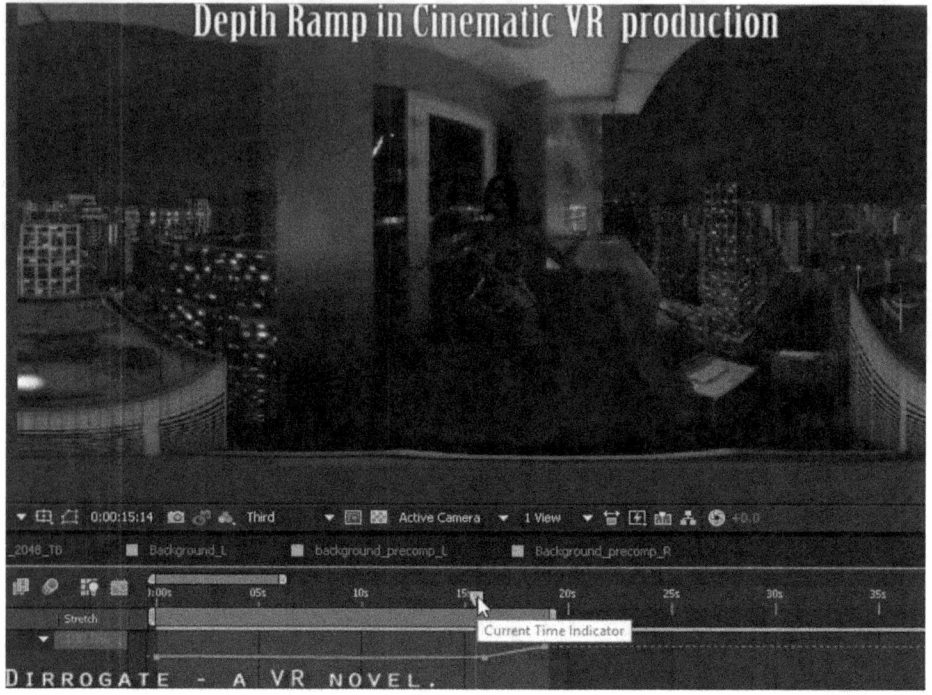

Bring out a pair of those old red-cyan anaglyph glasses and take a look at the image above. Next, follow it up by looking at the next image...

Depth Ramps In Stereoscopic Vr:

If you're reading the print version of this book type in the URLs below to download the images from the Internet archives [while

they're still hosted]
1) Image 1 - https://tinyurl.com/depthrampA
2) Image 2 - https://tinyurl.com/depthrampB

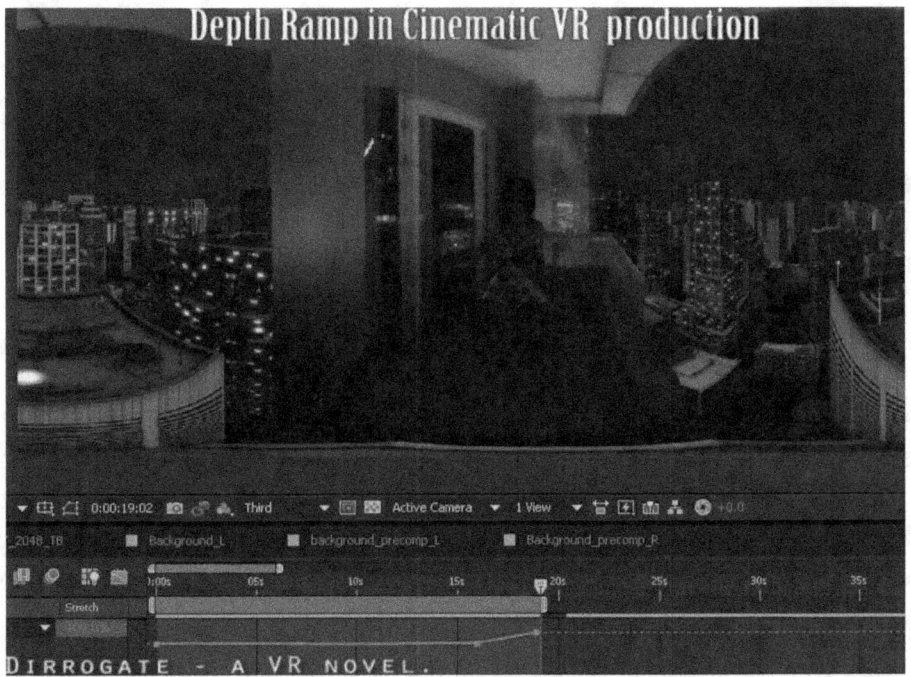

The images are the start and end frames of a "Depth Ramp."
In conventional stereoscopic 3D film production, a Stereographer
works first with the Director and the Cinematographer to plot out
a so-called depth script of how events (shots/scenes) will flow as
the narrative progresses. Directors who understand the potential
of what stereoscopic 3D can do for visual storytelling, can build
entire "mood scapes" where the subtle interplay between depth
budget and the scene being filmed can draw audiences into the
story.

For instance: Stereographers and Directors have been known
to inflate the depth budget of a scene in Hollywood 3D
movies to emphasize happiness, as well as contract the depth
budget on scenes depicting sadness or to heighten a feeling of

claustrophobia. Why and how is this relevant to Cinematic VR production?

Cinematic VR game engine driven Machinima, as well as stereo 3D live action VR capture can benefit from an understanding of the Depth volume (budget) in a scene. For the first time, visual story telling can take place on an Imax® like scale...where the cinema-screen is strapped to the audience's face. There is more than a fair chance that if depth budget is not paid attention to in a Stereoscopic 3D VR production, harm can come to audiences, ranging from mild headaches to (sometimes) severe nausea.

What Is A Depth Ramp?:

In a 3D movie, either conventional or Cinematic VR, the story usually flows sequentially and there will be a need to cut between scenes. Problems arise when the audience is viewing a scene of say, a first person Pov of an actor who's sitting at a desk watching a door at the far end of the room...followed by an immediate cut to a closeup of his hand pulling a gun from a drawer under his desk.

What happens is, the audience's eyes have converged (diverged actually) to 'fuse' the left-right images of the door at the far end of the room, and in the next shot they have to *instantly* converge to fuse the left-right stereoscopic image pair that forms the close-up shot. It does not matter whether this is filmed as live action stereoscopic VR or created in a game engine. To mitigate the possible hurt that will result in such a transition, stereographers (and now immersographers when it comes to Cinematic VR) usually employ a depth ramp within the span of one second; sometimes less, sometimes more, depending on the flow of the scene, where the outgoing shot will be brought "closer" to the audience and the incoming shot (of the hand) will start off at a further distance. Things will finally settle in at the chosen depth for the next shot after this "depth ramp" has been executed.

Now, there might be scenes where it most likely will be impossible to execute a drastic cut, even with a depth ramp. That's when a cat-in-the-window shot can/should be employed. Cat in the Window? - You know...that shot they have in movies that builds suspense or is used to cover-up a glitch when a bad take gets noticed only during post production?

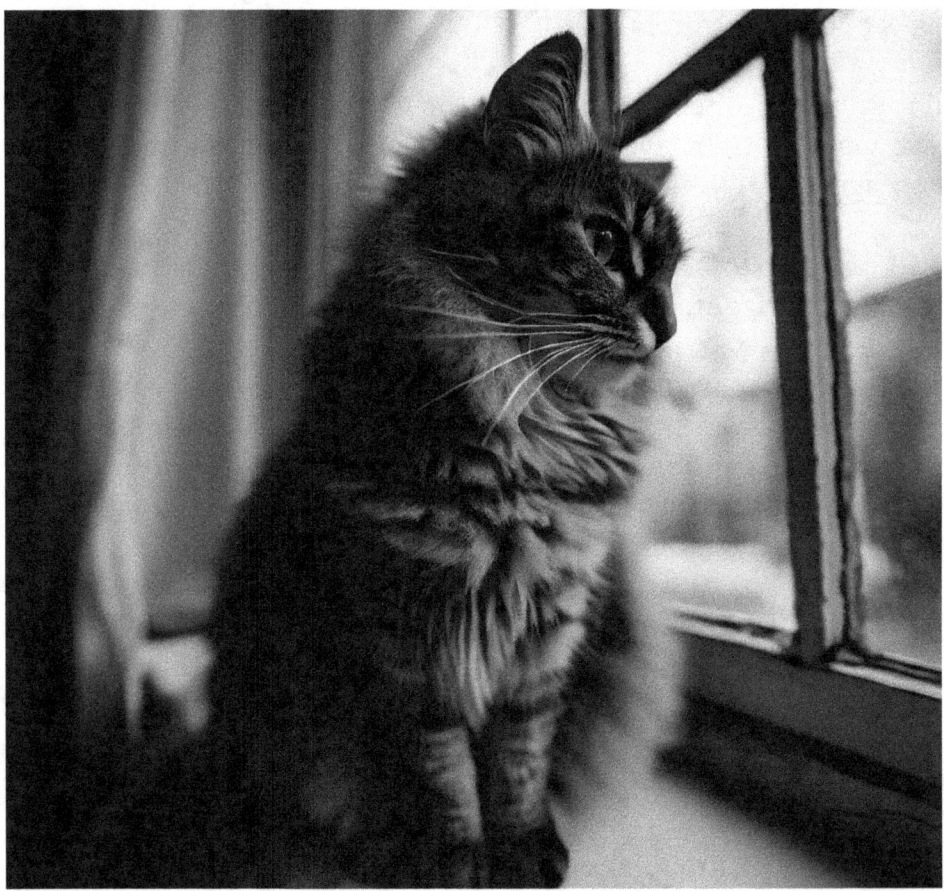

Well, that cat in the window shot, or clock-on-the-wall shot, when located at mid-depth in the 3D scene, can help soften the depth transition and visual gymnastics an audience's eyes have to perform when accommodating for the depth change from the door at the far end to the closeup of the hand picking up the gun from the desk.

Cinematic Vr Depth Ramp: How Is It Done?

Described below are the steps for a live action shot, though a similar technique can be applied to a Game Engine rendered VR movie. I've used Adobe After Effects but VFX artistes working with you the Immersive Storyteller, can use any of a number of VFX or editing software.

1) In After effects, apply the "offset" filter to either the left eye view or right eye view of the Stereoscopic Equirectangular footage.

2) Click the stopwatch icon to "animate" or keyframe the amount of H.I.T (horizontal image translation) that is required.

3) Over the span of about one second, slide the left image either to the left or right to move the "entire depth volume" of the current scene either direction; Negative Z space (out of screen) or Positive Z space (into the screen) such that the current scene will approximately match the depth of the next scene.

4) Rather than doing a simple depth ramp - it is advisable to meet the next scene halfway, i.e, apply a reverse depth-map to the next scene, so that it starts off half way closer to the depth of the current scene and then within a second settles in to the depth budget chosen for the remainder of that next scene.

Taking the example shot of Dirrogate, the VR motion graphic novel, shown at the start of this chapter, the scene is preceded by a flyby over a city, where the audience is floating over the rooftops of skyscrapers and then the camera 'lands' on the balcony showing a mid-closeup of the girl. The cut is abrupt and depending where the audience is looking (this is a 3D- 360 VR shot) we need to ensure the eyes have enough time to get accustomed to the environment.

We do this by starting the scene at a more comfortable depth, pushing the scene into positive Z space, and then transitioning toward the end of the scene, closer into negative Z space to where the next shot will start; a closeup of a comic book page containing this scene as a panel, flipping by. If red-cyan anaglyph glasses are not available, look at the position of the red fringe on the center-left pillar change, in the second image.

A word of Caution!

Depth ramps work best in Cinematic 180 VR films. They can certainly be employed in S3D 360 VR movies, but be aware of inflated (or deflated) depth in the hind (behind the viewer) 180 field of view while you execute a depth ramp in a 360 field of view movie. It's best to perform a depth ramp on narrative scenes where you're reasonably sure of keeping audience focus in the front half of the 180 field of view.

Mood Scapes? Emotion Engineering? Depth Script?...we can't be talking about depth ramps if we don't know what a depth script and depth budget is, right? Much less about "Emotion Engineering." Let's give it some space in the next chapter.

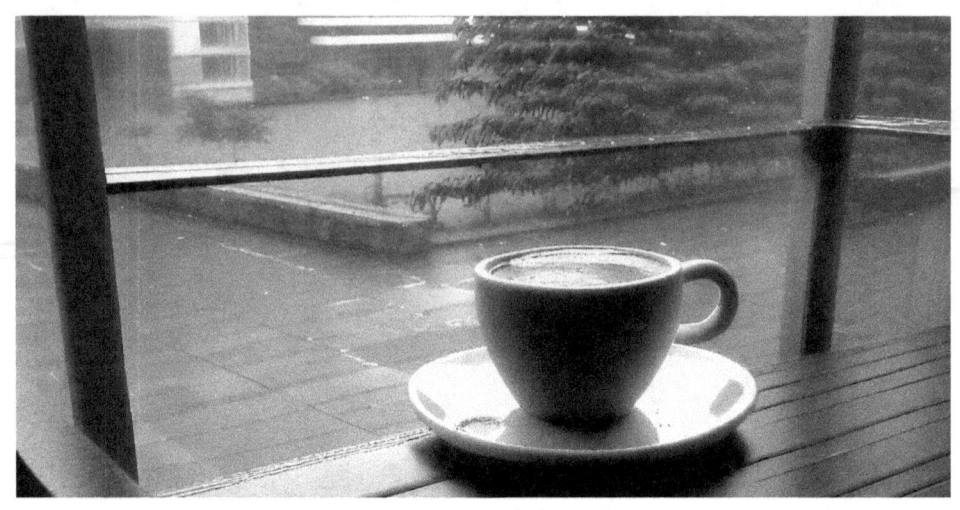

EMOTION ENGINEERING IN VR

W hat does the image above evoke in you? Chances are it creates a mood, or ignites familiar memories that cause an emotional reaction, however subtle, in your mind. Yet the image itself is a flat 2D representation of the real world.

We all know that VR movies are about immersing the viewer in a world, even if a fantasy one, such that the mind is tricked into suspending the feeling of disbelief, making the audience feel they are '*in the movie*.' The "depth channel" is unlocked in a stereoscopic VR movie, albeit, it's just an optical illusion. Depth can also be described as the spatial relation between different objects or subjects in a scene. Giving the eyes and brain access to this Spatial Information was previously impossible in 2D movies, and the closest attempts to do so were lateral movement of the camera to record parallax, or the use of depth of field. More astute Film Directors and Cinematographers (they are a dying breed thanks to rack-focus gizmos) use "deep staging" to recreate "depth"

Why...in every 2D movie, the most frequent reference made is how to give a scene that '3D look.' Now that we have the tech and the tools to do so, are we using it effectively? This discussion between us, aims to ask as many questions as it does to answer them and provoke thought on the effective use of depth in cinematic VR filmmaking.

Depth Script - In Narrative Vr Films.

It was very fashionable to use terminology such as depth budget and Depth script when 3D movie making was all the rage back in the 2010's. These were new terms coined, in an era where stereoscopic 3D movie-making was being rediscovered. What exactly is the need for a depth script? That can run into a few pages of theory and practical examples, but let's try to condense it a bit... A 3D feature film is approx 90 to 100 minutes long. A Cinematic VR film, I'd advise to be half as long in this first phase of Cinematic VR movie making, so as to acclimatize audiences to the medium. A depth script ideally shows the ebb and flow in a linear fashion, of the depth or shallowness of the 3D effect (realism?) in a scene, as the movie progresses. There can be a master depth script outlining the overall strength of the realism at different points in the movie, or a per character depth script in narrative feature films.

Depth scripts were also said to be used to craft the "mood" of a 3D film...Examples being, in a sad scene in the movie, depth should be flattened, in happy scenes...depth should be...well, fuller and deeper. Suggestions were also made that "inflating" depth on a subject such as the Protagonist or Antagonist in a movie, will lend more "power" to that character (I'm skeptical of this approach and relegate it as marketing gimmicks of 2D to 3D conversion studios.) Let's aim not to debunk any of these creative methods or theories, but instead, pose questions on the effectiveness or the non-effectiveness of them.

Should Sad Scenes In 3D Be Flat?

To me, this is a mixed bag answer, worthy of serious investigation using many scenarios before coming to a conclusion. For example, in real life if we are depressed and lying in bed on a gloomy and cloudy day looking out the window, would the world be compressed down like the layers of a popup get-well-soon card and be flattened down to the depth level of the windowpane? Or, would we still see a 3D world, which extends beyond the window, but with muted color? Another question that comes to mind; would it take us away from the immersion of the film, if subconsciously the brain is pre-occupied with a growing, nagging thought that something is not right with this compressed 3D world? It could be counterproductive for the Director if the audiences snap out of the unfolding story on seeing an abnormal use of depth in the scene.

Does a room go flat if you feel sad? The answer is no...*but,* we have to ask the question; When we are lost in thought, due to sadness or some such emotion, and we stare blankly out the window, or at an object at the far end of a room, are we really conscious of all the roundness of the world around us? In most probability our eyes are glazed, not really focusing on anything in particular, and indeed it could be said that the world goes "flat." Can the Director actually *engineer* this emotion in audiences via a VR film? Should they attempt to?

The Good Story Versus Technical Critique Experiment:

The easiest test of a well-directed movie is when you get into the movie from a point of view of evaluating it technically, but get lost half way into the movie; absorbed in the story, or at the very least, get distracted from your original task by the skilled acting and direction in the movie. A good story when coupled with good story telling ability will draw the audiences into the film, whether it's a 3d movie or not. We all know that a movie should not be made for 3D, and that 3D should be in the background, building the mood for the story.

Good camera work, acting, lighting and directing creates immersion. However, it can be argued that the very powerful optical illusion that is stereoscopic 3D...when used right, can supersede any of these other tenets of visual storytelling. After all, even without good camera work, acting, or directing, it's a real world (in the audiences mind) to roam around in. Therein lays the clue to the Director or Immersographer of whether they should or should not attempt to engineer emotions in audiences by playing with the depth of a scene.

When To Engineer Emotions With Creative Use Of 3D:

The Director can never be sure or over confident of their story telling ability. Despite best efforts, the outcome may not be as expected especially in a 3D VR movie. In 2D movies the audiences will rarely stray to examine the rest of the scene if the dialog is not gripping enough. In a 3D VR movie you can be *rest assured* they will. Even an insignificant lamp or chair or bookshelf in a scene will be more interesting and invite visual curiosity when the audience has lost interest in the acting or story.

Giving the audience "eye time-out" In a 20 to 45 minute Cinematic VR film, we have to make sure that audiences are not immersed in "deep 3D" from start to finish. This could be visually exhausting. Hence the Depth Script.
When engineering emotions or creating a mood with the use

of 3D, we *can* flatten depth and use a more conservative depth budget, but a suggestion would be to do that in combination with creative scene framing to absolutely be sure of not disrupting the suspension of disbelief. For instance: Start off with a conventional rounded depth budget for an interiors scene for a few seconds and then have the actors move towards or nearer zero-parallax distance to ease eye muscles (eye time-out). In a VR film as a rule of thumb, move the talent not the camera. Why? Because the audience *becomes the camera-person* when they wear the headset and your camera move no matter how stabilized you think it is, can cause nausea in many.

Switching from human GPU, to logic processing:
Borrowing from computer terminology...we can relax the audience's GPU (graphics processing unit..a.k.a the eyes) to allow their brains to process the plot unfolding by knowing when to creatively switch between deep 3D and a more subtle depth. To give another example: When a good DJ is performing at a nightclub, watch their routine. At some point they will gradually build up the tempo to near frenzy that will have almost the whole club on the dance floor.

Very talented DJs can hold the audiences till they are in danger of burning out, by seamlessly mixing one hit track after the other. However, a burnt out nightclub is no good and the night would end in a few hours, from exhaustion [and lack of bar sales!] They thus know the right time when to ebb the tempo and bring it up again. One wrong move and punters walk away from the floor.

Making the switch is an art-form and takes some talent to execute well in both 3D as well as VR movies. Suddenly deciding to "flatten" the depth of a scene simply because it's a sad scene, may "pull" the audiences out of the story. Timing it well, will make for a rewarding Cinematic VR experience.

I'll let you in on a little secret: As of the year of publication of this book, I'm still noticing many new-age Virtual Reality Immersographers and Filmmakers not knowing how to use or balance a Depth Budget. They shirk the pleasure of using positive Z space in the Cinematic VR films they create. Just by reading the previous chapter on Depth Ramping, you will know a lot more than them!

We should define an Immersographer at this point. They are evolved Stereographers who understand how to engineer emotions in audiences with the skilled use of stereoscopic 3D in VR storytelling. They work with the Director, Cinematographer and equally important, with the Editor, to create immersive Cinematic VR experiences.

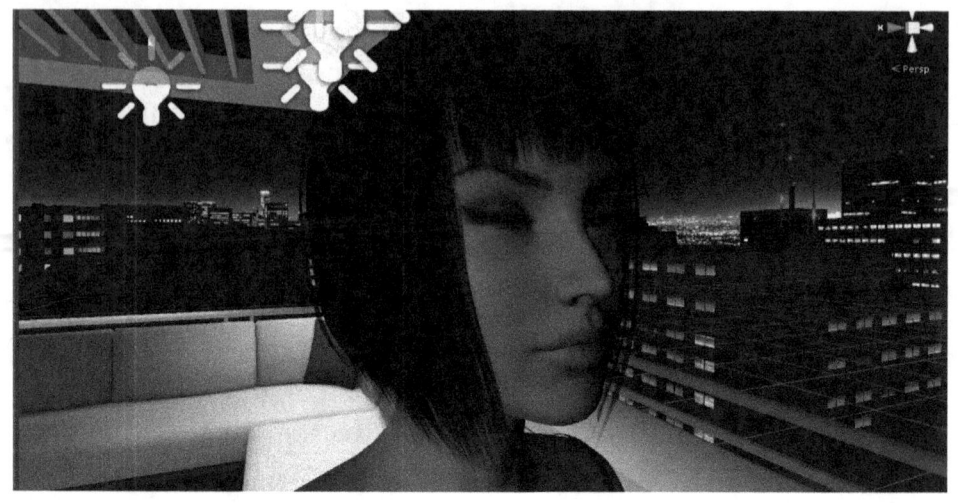

THE DILEMMA OF POSITIONAL TRACKING

EXT. DAN'S APARTMENT, TERRACE - NIGHT

(SFX: city sounds, a police siren wails in the distance)
We look at Maya through Dan's perspective, sitting on one of the sun loungers on the terrace.

MAYA
(stifling a yawn, stands up)
"It's getting late... Let's go inside?"

She stands up, but (we, the audience) Dan does not... And there's not much the Director can do about it, thus ruining his/her envisioned scene in this Narrative VR film. The culprit: Positional Tracking.

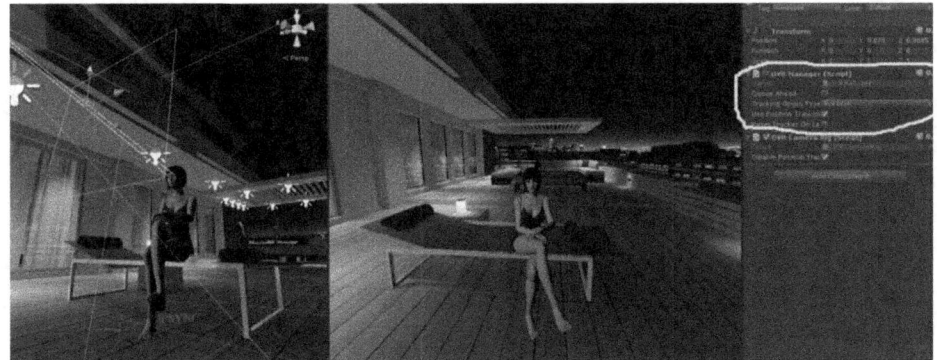

Positional Tracking: Or "Positracking" And Immersive Vr Filmmaking:

Before we dive in, let's recap the two kinds of virtual storytelling that's possible in Mixed Reality. There's the passive kind of VR video where the audience does not have 'agency' other than moving their heads around. This is called 3DoF (degrees of freedom) and is usually how we present video based VR content - shot stereoscopically, of course.

Then, there's the full 6DoF variety of VR story, where the scene is usually built in a game engine and the story, authored via a mix of interactivity and traditional linear filmmaking techniques. This latter way of narrative VR moviemaking is what we look at in this chapter. The sheer immersive nature of having an Imax® like screen strapped to audience's faces has new age filmmakers salivating at the prospect of using such a vast canvas to 'paint' their story on. As a medium in it's infancy, there's a temptation to get out there with 4 or 6 cameras and capture the whole 360 'stage' while framing action dead center and calling it a VR film.

It's only after one experiences 'spatial depth' along with the ability to look around, and with 6 degrees of freedom (rotation and position) does one come to appreciate the magnitude of what's possible via Cinematic VR.

The header image shows a scene from Dirrogate:DeepVR. PosiTracking can, arguably be called a cornerstone for defining interactive VR experiences. But...we're getting ahead of the plot. Let's back-track. The previous image has a circled part that reads (not very clearly) Tracking Origin: Eye Level. In the early days of VR authoring there were two choices in the Unity game engine for basing positional tracking of the headset (a.k.a audience position); Eye level and Ground Level.

If choosing Eye level, everything looked perfect and as expected. Wearing the headset, and having head-hopped into Dan's head, we the audience went from being a fly on the wall to now having First Person POV -something that is surprisingly quite natural in a VR film but could scream "amateur" if done in traditional narrative cinema. All would be fine until...

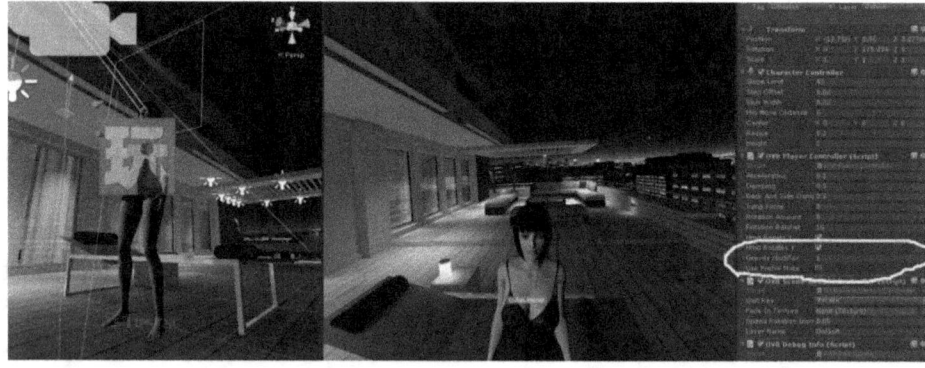

Maya stands up. Then, we'll find ourselves at the wrong height to look at her face as she speaks. The Director of course, wishes we stand up. But this is a film...a movie...and traditionally, movies were/are designed to be a passive entertainment experience, driven by a linear thread. Expecting someone to stand up when the actor does, would be a bit of a stretch. Additionally there's another (circled above) configuration; Use Profile Data.

When people first get their VR headsets they usually have to do a one-time calibration that 'locates' the user in 3D space and the ground in the real world. This allows the VR world to know if the user/player/audience is sitting or standing and the position of their head in 3D space.

This "user profile Data" is unique to each person using the headset and is stored in a file. The point being: a 6foot person will see the VR world from a different vantage point than someone of a different height. So if a 6 foot person were to stand, they would tower over Maya, our actor, and this angle is NOT what the Director might have in mind while 'framing' the scene (even though there are arguments that there's no such thing as framing for VR) So...

Scenario 1: Maya stands up, but the audience does not, thereby putting them at the wrong height for the remainder of the scene.

Scenario 2: Maya stands up, and so does the audience - but the user is 6 feet tall, thereby putting them at the wrong angle again.

Solution: Since we're authoring this movie in a game engine, we have a slew of tools at our disposal. One such tool is what I see as an essential plugin (for the Unity Game Engine) in the interactive storyteller's toolkit; Realistic Eye Movement. Despite its name, it does more than just eye movement and can intuitively, aided by some rudimentary A.I., move the actors head and torso to 'address' the location of the audience -the headset wearer.

In effect, if the wearer of the headset is 6 feet tall, Maya will look up at him while speaking. If the audience is sitting while she stands in the film, she'll look down. These settings can of course be fine-tuned and further, simple code can be added to randomize this interaction. Likewise, similar plugins would exist for Unreal Engine, the other interactive authoring platform for Cinematic VR filmmaking.

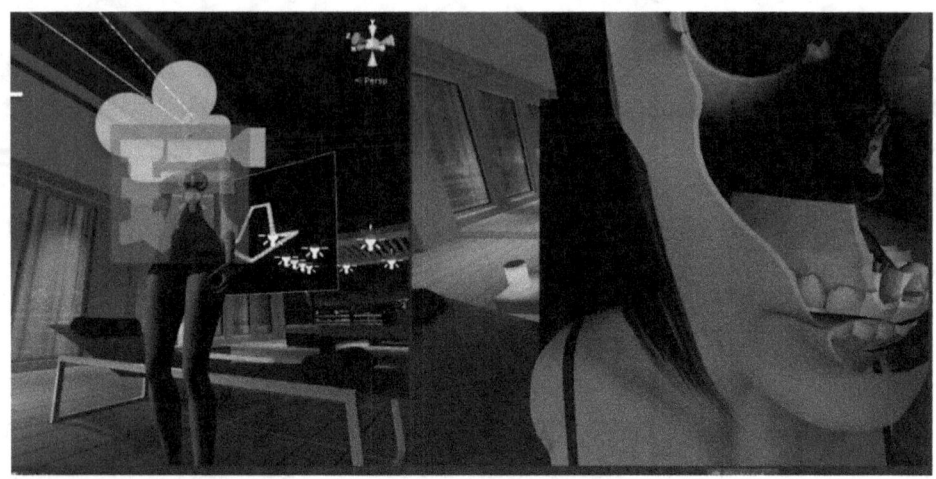

Say Ahhhhhh! - The bane of Positracking:

There is another highly undesirable side effect of using Positional Tracking - The Patrick Swayze, or Ghost Effect. Due to the less than optimal (in my opinion) way that positional tracking is implemented within game-engines, an audience can literally, lean into and see the insides of geometry. In the case of Maya, up-close, the audience can lean in and see her tonsils. There is interior geometry for the mouth because she speaks and even at a medium close-up distance, it would look unnatural to remove mouth geometry. Other areas where this un-desirable effect crops up is being able to stick one's head into walls and furniture.

There were crude workarounds suggested, such as fading the field of view to black when a collision is detected between the user (the camera) and geometry in the VR world, but I find it a less than optimal suggestion. So...What's a VR filmmaker who wants to go beyond shooting flat 360 video and calling it VR, to do? Once audiences experience what's possible with a true Hybrid VR film, there's every reason to believe Directors will have a hard time convincing themselves to fall back on vanilla 360 video VR when creating narrative XR films.

Hybrid VR films and Positional Tracking:
There is no denying it, filmmaking is evolving at a rapid pace. The VR cinematographer, filmmaker and Director will have to have at least surface knowledge of the tools and techniques of the trade, to appeal to new generation audiences.

Positional tracking will equally be important when shooting with volumetric camera systems. The way these systems work, is to capture human full motion performances from multiple synced cameras and then actual 3D geometry is extracted, optimized and textured to create a 3D actor performance ready to be imported into a CG world or a photogrammetry / Lidar captured real world set. If all this sounds daunting, rest assured as an emerging Filmmaker myself, it's a team effort in Cinematic Mixed Reality storytelling...just as it is in regular filmmaking.

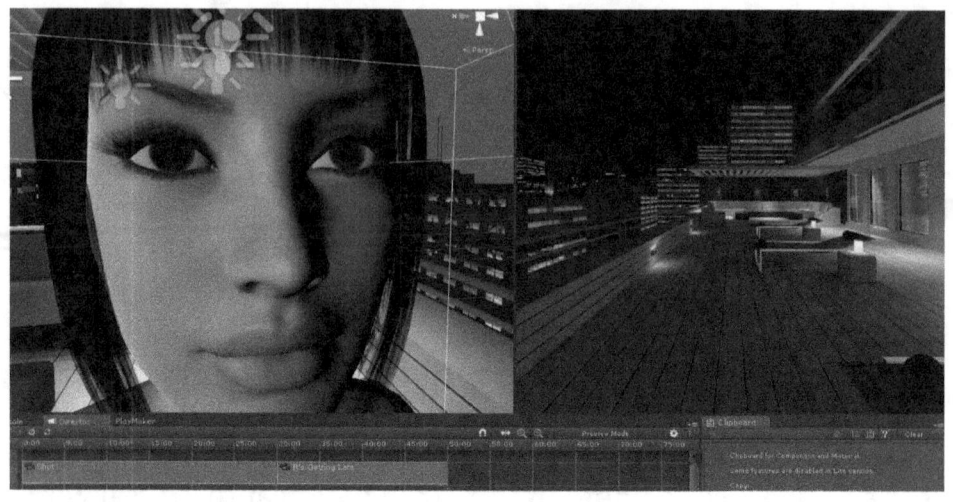

ROOT VR, DEEP VR AND
YOUR CAREER IN XR MOVIES

A few years ago I was shooting the opening scene of 'Dirrogate:DeepVR' at Hazelwood Terrace. The reason the scene shown above took long is not because Maya is a bad actor; no, in fact she's been really cooperative, going through multiple wardrobe changes, hair styles and contact lenses without fuss.

Learning the ropes of filming on Digital sets in Virtual Reality, and discovering a new language of storytelling along the way, is the reason. We'll get to some of the grammar and vocabulary soon; Deep VR and Root VR is in the title of the chapter after all. Let's talk a bit more about Digital Sets and working in this nascent industry, first.

Scene blocking in the Hollywood Metaverse?
HazelWood Terrace isn't a real world location as you've probably guessed by now. The location exists in VR, created by PolyBox. As VR and filmmaking in the Cinematic Metaverse matures, there is every reason to believe it will spawn a whole industry, just like its real world counterpart. Digital Sets and VR Studio backlots, Set designers, Costume and makeup, Digital actors -a whole virtual Hollywood will spawn online.

However, there are caveats. We aren't living in the Matrix, yet. The reason I could film Dirrogate:DeepVR, is only because Hazelwood Terrace was optimized for a generation of underpowered mobile VR platforms. Maya, our lead actress had to shed a few hundred thousand polygons to be
able to perform in the scene. She looked terrific and within the current decade, I'll wager, *in VR*, her appeal as a Digital Actor will grow 10 fold. "Presence" will be taken to new heights.

I'll go as far as to predict mass employment and job opportunities for many real world film industry professionals, provided they update their skill sets for The Cinematic Metaverse. To lend credence to the prediction, let's see what we need:
Cinematographers: those who understand Forward Lighting rendering, Gamma for VR displays, Differed rendering, Baking lightmaps along with their traditional realworld skills of three point lighting, etc.

Camera Persons: who understand the nuances of camera movement, Framing (yes there is such a thing) despite the lack of a proscenium, as we'll see later on in this chapter.

Set and Costume Designers: will need to familiarize themselves with creating digital replicas of real world materials, texture atlases and "substance designing" for digital satin, wood, leather.

Audio engineers and Music Producers: will need to upgrade their knowledge to take in Ambisonics, realtime environmental audio propagation and occlusion and in particular, because of the intimacy that a VR headset (theater) offers...ASMR.

A Director: will need to know how to leverage the limitations of the medium and throw the rule book out the window. They might also demand that the location or set have Root VR and Deep VR capability. It's important to have a firm grasp on what's involved in Cinematic VR filmmaking, and how to create an experience that surpasses the reason audiences currently go to the cinema -that of wanting to get away from the rigors of real life to experience a virtual one.
It's part of the evolution of Cinema as we know, where filmmaking will be hybrid - A mix of real world photography and the total immersion that is possible when merged with synthetic reality. We could even have the real world as a set! (Mixed Reality movies.) Which brings us to discussing the main topics of this chapter...What is ROOT VR?

While shooting at a VR location such as Hazelwood Terrace, the Director might ask if everything is Root VR ready. Let's see what that entails. Is the physics in place? Does the sun-lounger and terrace furniture for instance, have mass as their real world counter parts would?

What happens if the audience - the person wearing the VR headset, climbs up on the rail around the terrace?
Where is this place - does the story/narrative dictate that the location be tied to a real-world latitude and longitude and weather system? Does it have a functional time of day system - Passage of time in VR can be manipulated to great effect than is possible in traditional Cinema. This feature has to be wielded responsibly. These are some of the fundamentals of what we'd call "Root VR" - a term I'm borrowing from computing terminology - giving the

Director "super user" status to craft the narrative.

When offering VR locations on lease for filmmaking, a VR Location Scout might look for these assets to be tabulated. In case it's not obvious - The following image is of the famous Hazelwood Terrace, being prepped for a shoot. Unlike in the real world, "Golden hour" in Hybrid VR filmmaking, along with the weather, can on-demand, be manufactured by the Director.

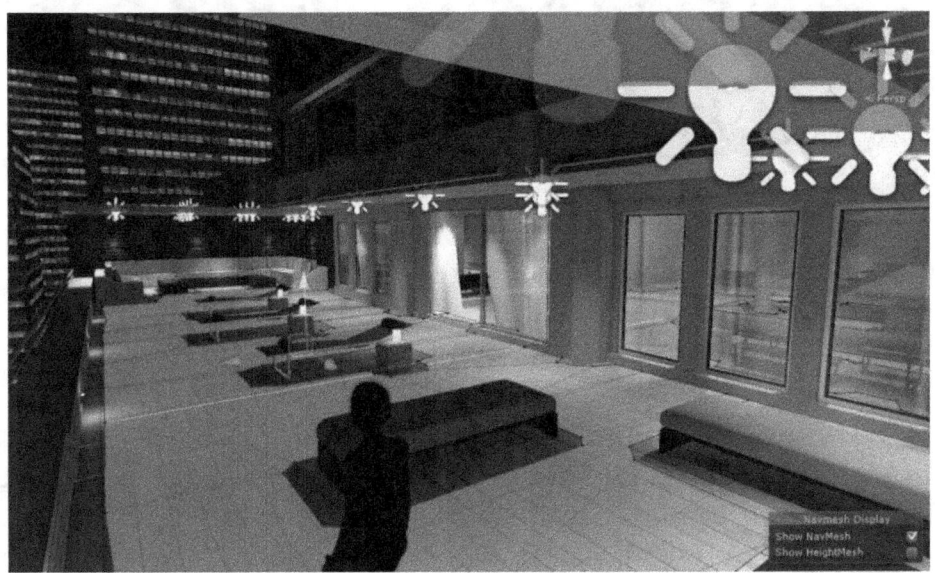

What is DEEP VR?
While Root VR allows access to the metal edge-rail at Hazelwood Terrace, the Director, using their discretion and depending on if the narrative is multi-threaded, might decide to not allow the audience the liberty of committing VR suicide. The blue areas [light grey grid in the print version of this book] are what the Director has marked as "navigation safe" in this scene, both for the actors and the audience present in the movie. In a larger scene, perhaps a Hazelwood VR backlot, or Digital town, an entire city block could be nav-meshed to allow crowds of standee VR actors to walk around, autonomously. A normal Cinematic VR film (shot

with a 360 camera) by its nature, is challenging to 'direct', given that the audience is free to turn and look around. Things go up a notch or two on the directorial scale for a Hybrid VR film where the audience might be allowed physical locomotion on the set. How Deep can/should Deep VR go?

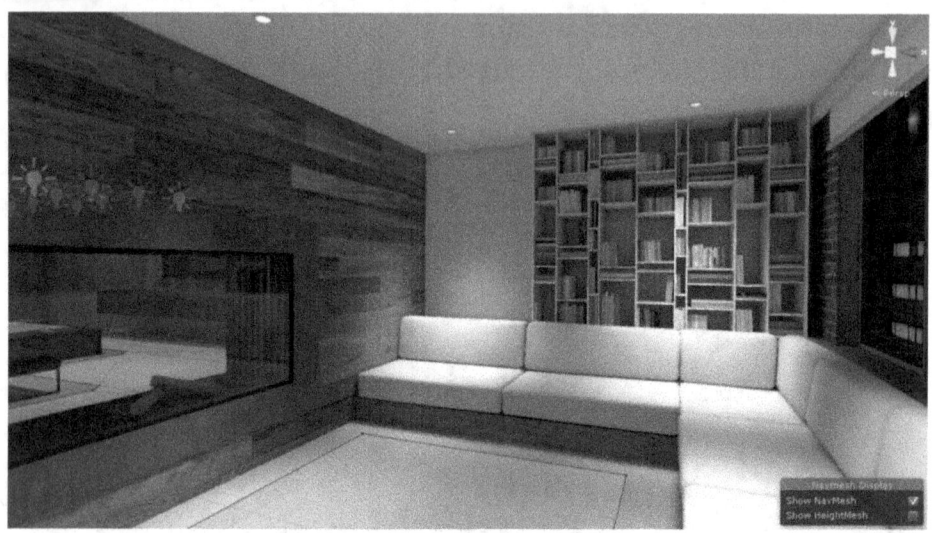

In the scene above, the nav-mesh shows that the audience won't be able to reach the book-shelf. If they could, the Director might want to make it so every book can be picked up, and contain readable material. Consider this:

In Dirrogate:DeepVR, ideally the Terrace scene would end with Maya saying, "It's getting late... let's go inside." At which point she walks into the living room. The audience is free to follow her or - walk around the terrace exploring the area taking in the night-scape, or watch aircraft lights blinking as they come in for a landing. This is not important to the narrative, but builds atmosphere; a subliminal form of that coveted word in VR...Presence.

So, how do we pick up the narrative?

The moment the audience *does* enter the Living room, they are allowed a few steps before they 'trip' a scene change trigger. [We're talking interactive authoring of a Cinematic VR film via a Game Engine in this case] An invisible 3d object that when collided with by the wearer of a VR headset, causes the scene to fade to black and moves to the next scene in the narrative, which is the bedroom and Maya's internal monologue as from the original Dirrogate VR film.

At this point the audience does not have access to the living-room study and the bookshelf. However, after Maya's interior monologue, they could (The Director decides how deep, the DeepVR should be) leave the bedroom and walk to the book shelf, pick up a book that should have real rendered text on its pages. How deep? The Director might ask that 20 books be on the shelf and contain real literature. The audience can read...in VR, till dawn. The scene would then fade out, eventually to the next scene as intended in the original narrative. If the physics were left intact by the Director, the cushions could be picked up and tossed around, the books scattered around the floor...but in the name of all things holy in filmmaking...I digress.

The point is, in a Cinematic DeepVR film, we are aiming at total immersion. Toward that end, even the texture of fabric of the cushions, the wood paneling and the paint texture of the wall, count. This can be a blend of realworld photography and synthetic conversion.

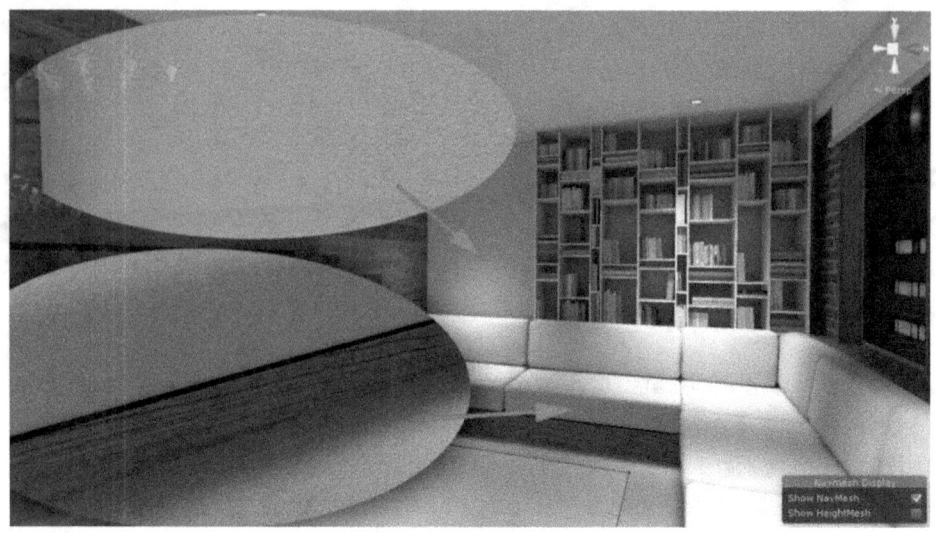

A testament to the finesse of the Hazelwood Loft set is, the fine level of detail. The picture above does not do justice to the feeling and an urge it gives rise to, when experiencing the room via a VR headset - that of wanting to reach out and touch the wall and fabric. Where Polybox have excelled, is in having this set run even on the low end mobile VR devices. No mean feat! Today, there exists far more 'realistic' real world scanned sets [Digital replicas] for use in hybrid VR filmmaking.

What is Hybrid VR?
As we've seen before, a debate rages on the topic: Is Cinematic VR really VR? One camp has gamers, who by nature, inhabit a completely synthetic world. They have experienced the joy of "positional tracking" -something that's not currently possible with stereoscopic 360 video capture of a scene. While everyone who can currently afford a 360 camera rig claim they are producing VR, I'm of the opinion, that at minimum, an experience needs to be stereoscopic 360 to coerce an audience's brain into 'immersion.'

Yet -even I'll admit, the way forward is to blend real world (stereoscopic) 360 photography with CG to qualify for the VR label. Eventually we'll all be producing narrative VR experiences that are either entirely synthetic reality, or a mix of stereoscopic 360 photography and CG.

In the case of Mixed Reality stories, we'll include the real world around us, as part of a Cinematic XR Metaverse experience.

Eventually, developments such as Lightfield technology at cinematic frame-rates, will afford a more advanced option. Today's Lidar and photogrammetry and NerF capture, already allow for bringing the real world into the realm of synthetic reality, albeit not in real time. As a side note: Have a look at some of the good work RealityVirtual [https://www.realityvirtual.co/] are doing. Documenting real world locations and preserving history, digitally. Such *Digital backlots* are fascinating to me, if used in storytelling.

Dirrogate: DeepVR:
Earlier on I'd mentioned a need to understand Camera placement. While it's true many of the rules of traditional cinematography either do not apply or need to be re-written, as it currently stands, there's a need to know about Camera placement in a Hybrid VR film.

Two currently well-known engines for Hybrid VR filmmaking are Unity and Unreal Engine. CryEngine is a formidable contender, and worth investigating. However, I've for now, I've settled on Unity. The thing with Game Engines and current VR hardware limitations is: Polygon count and frame-rate. As it stands, even with just Maya in the scene, it ruled out creating Dirrogate:DeepVR as a film playable on mobile VR headsets. Optimizing the geometry destroys Maya's 'realism' even further. I'd barely managed the recommended 90 frames per second, with the terrace, the living room and Maya visible in the shot.

This is where camera placement comes in. Occlusion Culling and Frustum Culling! [A reminder: Does a Mixed Reality Storyteller or Director need to know all this? Yes, but even surface knowledge helps. Immersive Filmmaking is the same as regular filmmaking - it's a team effort!] The way the scene was staged, it put Maya in the corner of the terrace, with us (the camera) aimed at her and far off buildings in the background. The buildings have a very low polygon [geometry] count.

If, for instance, the scene was blocked such that Maya stood in the doorway near the curtains, and we had our backs to the terrace rails looking at her and taking in the whole terrace and the living room...the polygon count of the scene would be at its maximum, thereby dropping frame rate in a realtime rendered hybrid movie. Game Studios are masters of this art in regular game worlds, but might still be learning when it comes to VR and Mixed Reality.

Getting back...With Maya in the corner of the Terrace facing us and just low polygon buildings in the background, if we now turn the camera around [our heads in the VR headset] to view the living room, Maya will be out of the field of view of the camera and so not be rendered by the Game Engine. Advantage Frustum culling! Not maintaining at least 90 frames per second, which is the recommended/mandated frame rate for a good VR experience, can lead to strain and an unpleasant experience for audiences.

The go-to solution to remember? "Frustrum culling" a term that VR filmmakers and DoPs may soon be spouting, is one weapon. The game engine also eliminates rendering any geometry that is hidden (occlusion culling) by a larger object in front of it. Intelligent camera placement and scene blocking is a skill needed in realtime Cinematic VR filmmaking, as we're all discovering.

We haven't talked about the ethics involved with Digital actors.

Questions and observations such as these come into play:

- How close should the Director allow the audience to get to the Digital actors? In Dirrogate:DeepVR there was a decision taken of not enabling physics on the clothing of the actors. This is important, because audiences with hand tracking or VR input devices such as the (ironically named) Touch controller, would not stray too far from the intent and narrative.

- When the audience gets too close to Maya, she either turns away or, if you are playing Dan, the main character, (there's head-hopping in the film) she might reciprocate with a smile or other friendly gesture.

Hybrid VR filmmaking might sound intimidating but it's worth repeating: It isn't essential to master every aspect, unless you are an indie filmmaker. Film-making is still a collaborative effort, and brings together talent specializing in different fields. There's no need to learn coding or computer graphics per se, but awareness and creative-tech knowledge is important... as is food for thought for filmmaking in the Cinematic Metaverse.

PART 3 - CINEMATIC XR STORYTELLING

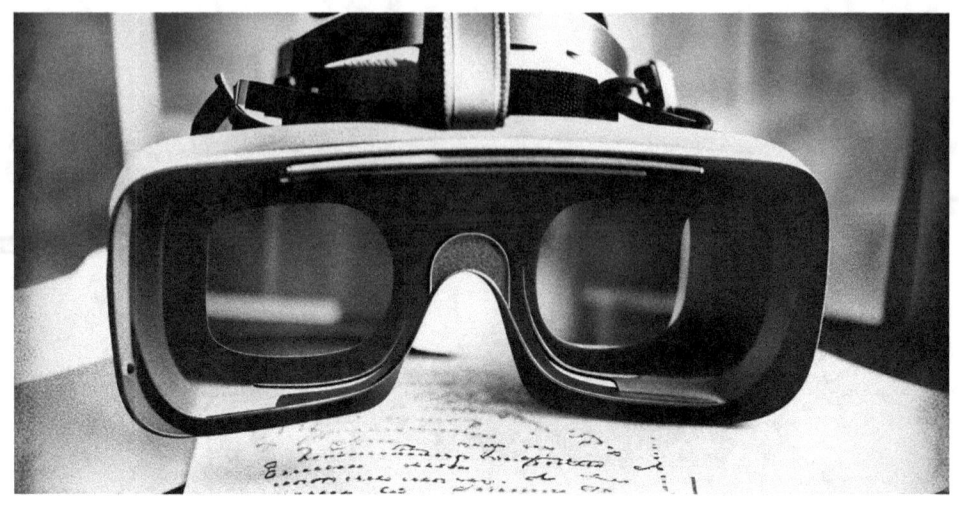

SCREENWRITING FOR CINEMATIC VR FILMS.

I s there such a thing as writing a screenplay for VR? While it may sound intriguing to announce: "I'm writing my next epic for a 3D-VR movie", should we be making movies for 3D or making movies in 3D?

To what extent does screenwriting affect the outcome of a Theatrical 3D or for that matter, a Cinematic VR movie?
These are all un-answered questions, but we can try and answer them by first defining a "log line" (to borrow a screenwriting term) for what an immersive VR film is all about. Stereoscopic 3D-VR thrives on:
1. Details or detailing
2. Dwell time [Book: Think in 3D, page 51]

The reason 3D (yet again) got a lackluster reception, was because the above two ingredients were sorely missing in the slew of 3D movies that came out as Hollywood tried to cash in on making an extra buck on tickets. It's probably due to residual thinking ...2D thinking... by Directors and Cinematographers. One can't blame them.. there was a whole lot of un-learning to do and not many established professionals wanted to go back to film school. In my opinion, take movies such as The Transformers for instance...Those mechanical monsters were exquisitely detailed, the gears, mechanics etc...but did the audience get a chance to savor the detailing in 3D? How about the cutting (edit) pace of 3D movies? Again, artefacts of 2D movie-making at play.

There's always the complaint that action movies cannot have time to show details or "dwell" on a shot or scene. I beg to differ. Case in point, The Matrix. It has amazing action, yet had beautiful dwell time (all those slo-motion bullet time shots) and the movie was 2D! Those are the shots/scenes that would have looked exquisite had the movie been shot in 3D. Does it mean that all action scenes in 3D should now ape The Matrix? No, but there needs to be at least some dwell time inserted, perhaps "craftily," by the screenwriter.

The Crafty Screenplay writer.

By learning what works in 3D and in VR...it allows the screenwriter to visualize scenes better, and utilize Virtual Reality as the medium to tell the story and draw the audience *into* the film. The scenes themselves do not have to be Matrix like. What's missing sorely today in Virtual Reality films, is the lack of use of proper 3D to depict *human emotion*.

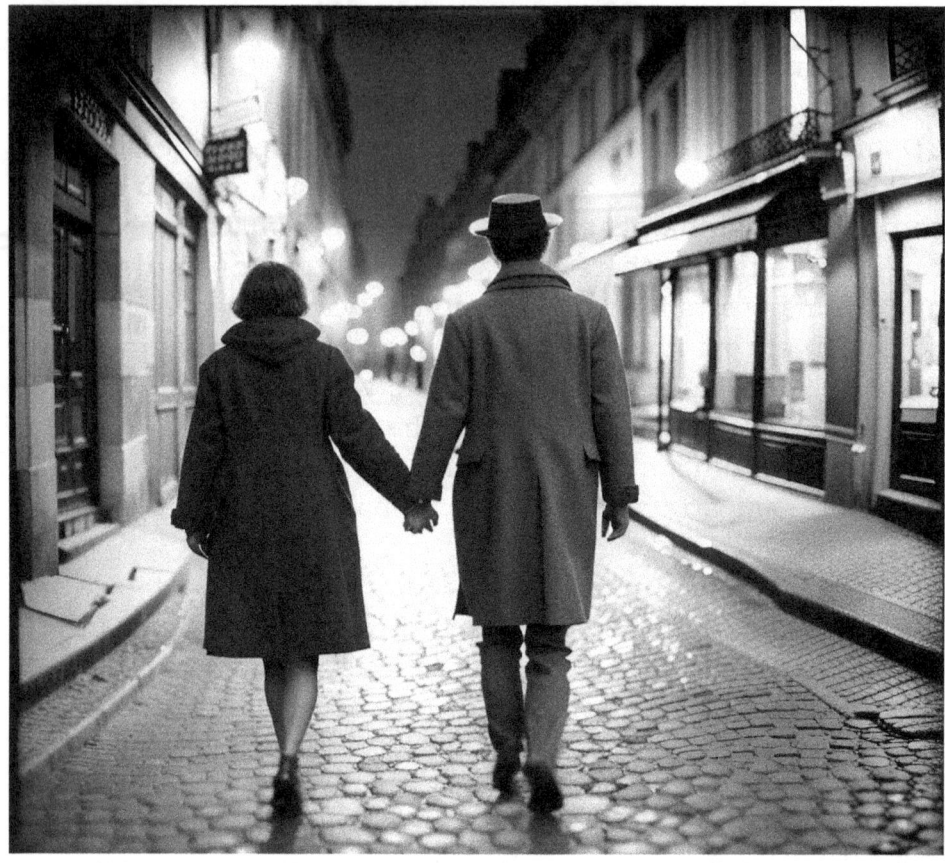

Midnight in Paris - If this movie was commissioned as a Cinematic VR film or a 3D film for theatrical release (remember we can extract a DCI compliant Cinema 3D format movie from a VR film), how would we immerse the audience in a romantic late evening stroll on cobbled stoned streets down a winding path on the banks of the river Seine? This is where the screen writer could weave in some crafty 'detailing' into the story... Say the character is absentmindedly flipping a coin as he strolls and it falls. We can show him picking it up and then walking along.

Motivation for this action? - *It's his lucky coin!-* Without having to type in CLOSE ON, or ANGLE ON, the DoP will have to lower the camera angle so the actor can pick the coin. Result?...A closer view of the pavement and those (maybe wet with recent rain) cobbled stones, is what might bring back memories to the audience or, transport them to that location in your VR film, for the very first time. Now, add in the 'scrunch' of mud on the cobbled stones in Ambisonic VR audio...and you have a whole differet level of immersion.

Those brief moments where the eye can linger, can savor... is where the use of immersive VR excels.

A close-up of a character wiping away a tear from another actors face...seen by the audience, up close... The "relief" and contours of the skin of a human face presented in 3D, draws the viewer into your story, as though they are right there with the character. These are scenarios that the screenwriter can weave into the story without actually spelling the shot and camera angle to the Director or DoP. We know a screenwriter should not suggest camera angles to established Cinematographers or pacing to the Director. What a screenwriter can do is, cleverly weave stereo3D into the story in such a way that it's natural yet has those 2 ingredients. Detailing and Dwell time.

How do you write a screen play for an action movie in 3D that won't make it boring? and yet have detailing, dwell time and "Eye Time Out?" Eye Time out is explained on page 45 in the book: Think in 3D. If you can find the official trailer of the movie, Matrix Reloaded, at around the 47 second mark into the video, is your Dwell Time and eye-time out that's executed rather well, before the pace picks up again. The trick would be in the screen play, to mention:

"...and Trinity lands on her feet like a sleek, black cat".

Otherwise the pacing and framing would be left open to

interpretation by the Director or Cinematographer.

Character Arc and The Depth Script:
Screenplays have a Character Arc and Stereoscopic 3D and Narrative VR movies have a Depth Script. A screenwriter can leverage the concept of a Depth Script when building their Character Arc. The general premise of a Depth Script is a visual graph that the Stereographer or Immersographer and DoP uses to chart the progress of the "3D ness" of the movie as it plays out. More creative use of depth scripts encompass:

Sad scenes having a "shallower" depth, while happy moments allow the Immersographer to "dial up the depth". This handling of depth is of course an art in itself and experienced Immersographers and Directors work in tandem to achieve it for maximum "presence." It can, if done well, add to the immersion and suspension of disbelief in the movie. The concept is discussed to some extent in the chapter on Depth Ramping, in this book, and was first introduced in the book: "Think in 3D."

Beautiful synergy between Director, Immersographer and Screenwriter can come about, if the Character Arc and Depth script work together. In brief, a depth script takes into account the ebb and flow of Depth in the movie, to add immersion, but also serves other much needed and crucial purposes, such as to prevent audience eye-strain, to match between cuts in scenes and more. While the Screenwriter will have no way of knowing what the depth script would be, the intention here is to make the writer aware that a Character Arc combines well with a depth script to build the "mood" of scenes as the character (protagonist / antagonist) traverses the beats of the screenplay.

Backstory in Stereo3d?

Can flashbacks and backstory benefit from the play of depth (happy childhood memories = more depth, loss of a loved one, flatten the depth). This will no doubt be the job of the

Immersographer and the depth script, but it's mentioned here so that the screenwriter can be aware of how stereo3D can influence even if at a subconscious level, some emotion in the viewers. Flashbacks usually have a slower pace, even when recounting car crashes and such. These are "visual bites" that 3D was made for. We're using "3D" here, because it's *a faithful recording of spatial depth* - which tricks the brain into believing the audience is really there as a witness to the story unfolding

Above are only some guidelines. There are certainly other areas that a screenwriter, delving into the medium of storytelling in Virtual Reality can explore. A screenplay writer can be a great asset to a film by planting seeds to help the Immersographer, right there in the screen play. The more the screenwriter learns about the medium, the more they can leverage Stereoscopic 3D in their screen play, which in turn makes for a more engaging experience for the audience.

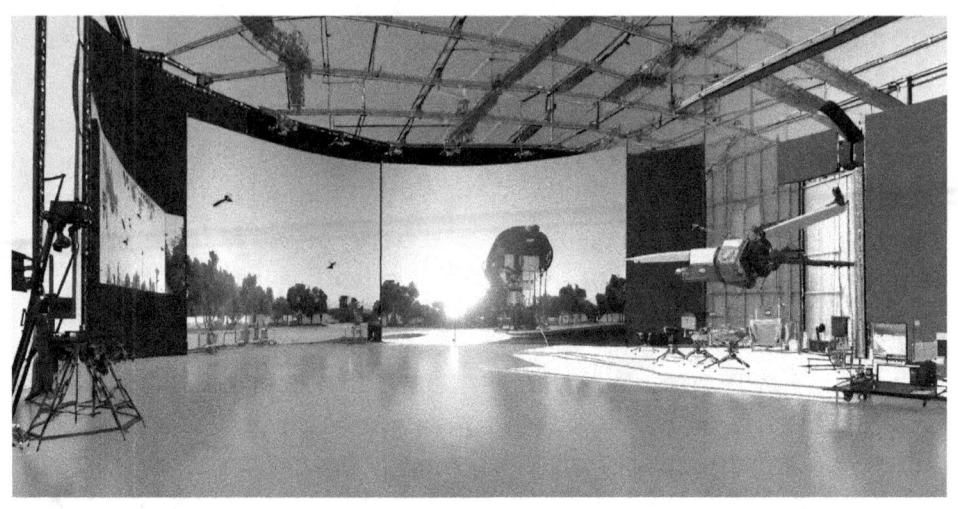

VIRTUAL PRODUCTION TO CINEMATIC VR FILMS

During the Covid '19 pandemic of 2020, the entire film industry came to a grinding halt. Major films had to halt production because of the contagion.

That situation gave rise to the popularity of using massive LED walls arranged in sound stages driven by a minimal crew. "Virtual Production" is not new. The old fashioned way of doing it existed in the form of green screen cycloramas and scene tracking. Then with the advent of finer resolution LED panels which could be stacked to create a 'wall,' a few films and TV productions started using Virtual Production techniques because of the cost and time savings that could be had over the logistics of multi-location shoots. Game Engines such as Unreal Engine became the standard to create these "virtual environments" which could be a mix of spherical video and/or Computer Generated [CG] worlds. The big advantage touted by LED based Virtual Production is that there's 'natural' lighting on the actors, cast by the LED panels themselves as well as giving the actors visual cues to perform better since they're immersed in a visual environment and not staring at green paint. What has this got to do with Cinematic VR filmmaking?

Food For Thought: Crossover Films In Xr

The clue is right there in the title. Normally, Virtual Production is used in regular 2D filmmaking. To the best of my knowledge at the time of this book being published, there's not yet been any stereoscopic 3D movie filmed on any of the many Virtual Production "Volumes" (read: sound stages.) Yet, and you'll probably be reading it here first: There's a way to record stereoscopic 3D footage from high-end Virtual Production Stages. This also has benefits for VR and AR extensions to the film...but we're jumping ahead. Getting back...what's needed is:

- High refresh rate LED panels.
- An LED processor capable Frame Remapping.
- Genlocked pair of Cameras.

Now, while modern high-end LED processors support a so-called 'Frame Mapping' technique. Its purpose and intent is usually to *simultaneously* shoot two unique angles off of the same LED screen with actors in front, with two different genlocked cameras. But, two cameras is exactly how stereoscopic 3D is captured! Having the main cameras shoot the talent in front of the LED screen stereoscopically, in sync with stereoscopic visuals being displayed on the LED wall behind (that's where Frame remapping comes in)...gives us in-camera, final pixel captured, stereo film!

Still with me? Hang in there! Now imagine instead of projection a stereoscopic background environment on the LED wall using this frame-remapping technique, one was to alternate between flat green color every other frame. Green light-spill is a concern but can be mitigated with the "timing" of the frame rate and frame remap.

The result is, we get both, a visual for the actors to help in their performance along with a 'matte' for later keying out the talent (actor) who could then be inserted into a VR scene -or for that matter- an AR / Mixed Reality scene, as part of a cross-over Cinematic XR movie.

In some flavors of game-engine authored VR movies, live actors are inserted as 'camera facing billboards' into the scene. If they were shot stereoscopically, *the illusion of rounded depth is very, very high*. The CG set created in the Game Engine that drives the Virtual Production Volume is just a Digital Asset that can be optimized and used for the cinematic VR cross-over version of the film.

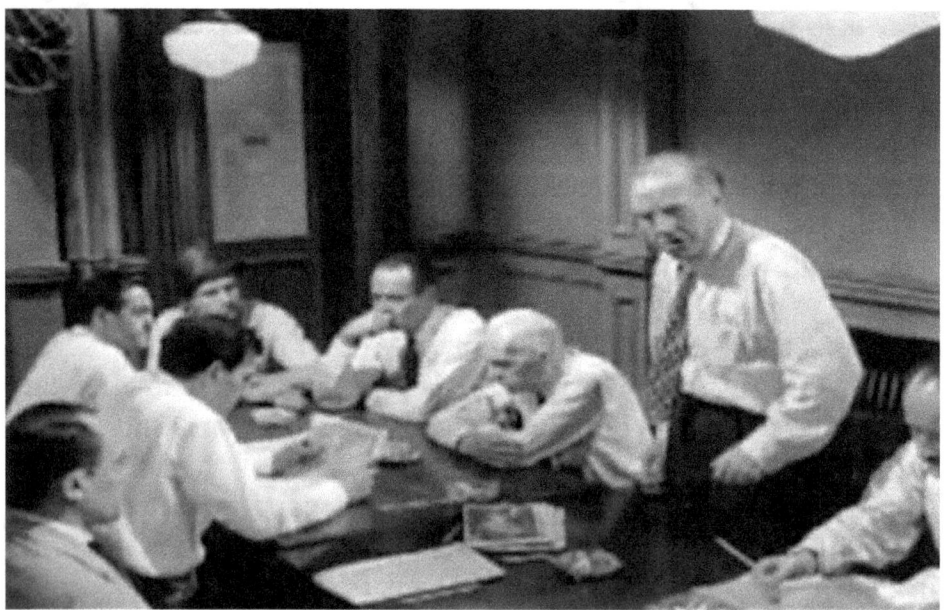

Twelve Angry Men in Your Living Room.

Whole Augmented Reality scenes can be extracted via Virtual

Production methods. One way is to use the green matte method along with the Game engine billboard method. This would suffice for a 3DoF POV kind of XR film extension where one or more characters, *breaks the 4th wall* to enter audience-space, during a hybrid 2D / AR movie playing in a headset.

Mixed Reality story extensions of regular movies will be in demand, on new generation XR headsets.

Such AR or Mixed Reality productions could be factual stories where a host *steps into your living room* to address you...or how about a remake of 12 Angry Men, where you have a choice of watching the classic in your VR headset in big-screen format, or have them debate at a large table right there in your living room!

Another way is to use an optimized version of a CG set created for the LED 'volume' itself, and then film actors wearing motion capture suits, who later get replaced by CG actors in a Mixed Reality version of a scene. This affords the audience full 6DoF freedom to 'walk around' the scene unfolding in their living space.

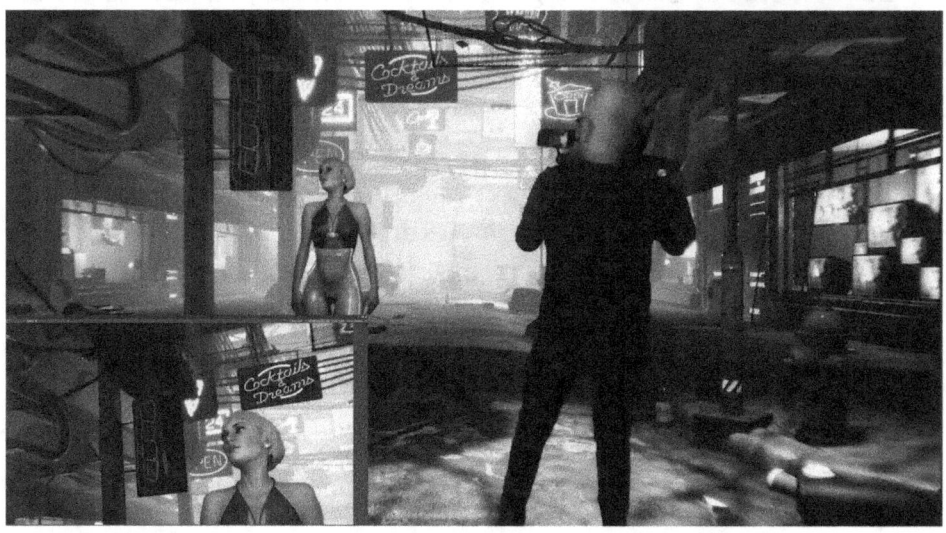

Virtual Production beyond LED Stages:

Certain sections of Hollywood decided to hijack the term "Virtual Production" to exclusively refer to the craft of shooting scenes in an LED volume/stage. Virtual Production goes much further than shooting actors and subjects in front of wall sized LED panels. In the previous image, *I'm inside a CG set** shooting a CG actor for what will eventually be a conventional 2D or 3D movie. The device I'm holding is a standard shoulder rig with a VR tracking device on it. That device's XYZ location in the real world, is calibrated and linked to a 3D game engine's camera. It's a similar concept to what Directors such as James Cameron and Jon Favreau use when shooting CG films.

The inset close-up box in the image is the part of the scene I 'see' on a viewfinder that's on the shoulder rig. There's also Focus and Zoom controls on the shoulder rig. They change focus and zoom *of the Game Engine's camera.* The "take" or shot contains a more natural feel that Directors and Cinematographers prefer, versus an animator keyframing the CG camera's path across the duration of a shot. The interesting part is, as the camera move performed by the Director or Cinematographer is 'digitized', infinite takes are possible, *after-the-fact*, with new focus and zoom settings, and the whole move is repeatable ad infinitum, while animation crew change the character's moves, expressions, clothes etc...

Lastly, Virtual Production encompasses even simple green screen production tech, where actors and props are filmed and the footage later composited as (stereoscopic 3d) billboards, in a VR or Mixed Reality production.

----

* *I'm standing in front of a green screen. The image is a final composite used in an instructional video.*

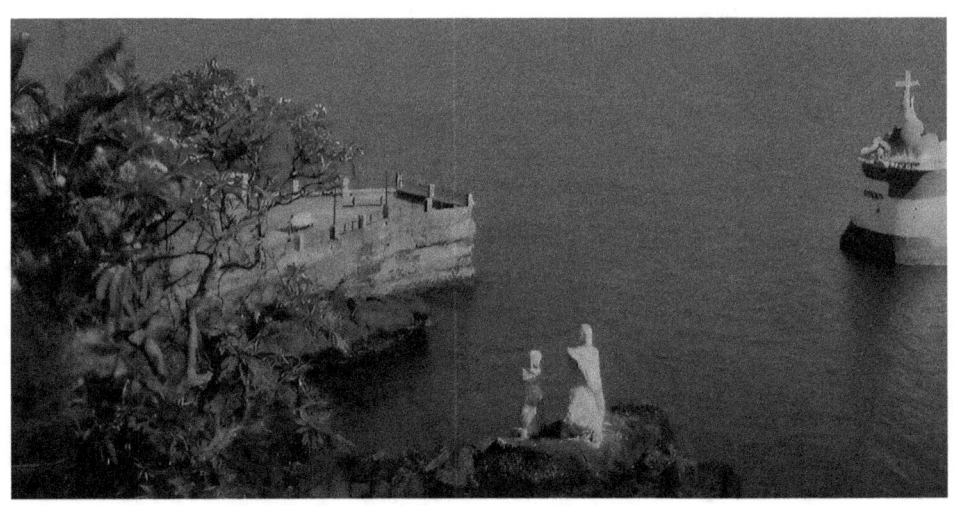

DONAPAULA: AN XR
SHORT FILM

DonaPaula, the Portuguese-Goa folktale is a fascinating one, steeped in myth and lore. One version of the story states that Dona Paula (real name Paula Amaral) jumped off or was thrown off the cliff into the sea wearing only a pearl necklace, given to her by her lover.

Legend has it that on a full moon night she emerges from the ocean wearing the pearl necklace and roams the nearby village, looking for her lover, or to exact revenge. Perfect! I felt...toying with the idea of writing a short story in screen play format. Doing further research on Dona Paula, I learnt her tombstone was identified somewhere in the early 2000's and the full moon appearance part of the legend sounded great for a location based

AR extension to the VR short film.

Let's break-down the screenplay to see how we might translate it into a Cinematic XR short film.

EXT.DONA PAULA JETTY, GOA, DUSK (MOONLIT)

The night is setting in as the last few couples leave the pier. We stand by the edge of the rail looking out at sea, each passing moment it gets more 'night' and the Moon grows brighter.

FADE OUT/IN

Still on the pier, our POV opens to a rocky outcrop with
a distinct whitewashed statue... we hear
PAULO (V.O.)
(who is us in VR)
This place... so familiar.

CUT TO:
Third person POV shows Paulo raising his head, squinting and lifting a pair of binoculars to his eyes.

CUT TO:
POV of Binocular masking, looking at closeup of the statue. Then, behind us (using positional audio) a soft soothing female voice...
DONA PAULA (V.O.)
That Statue...They were lovers, you know.

FADE IN SLOW: 360
We (PAULO) turn to see a beautiful woman, mid 20's, wearing her hair in an elegant roman braid, casual white translucent top and skirt, smiling.

PAULO
Oh! I didn't know anyone was here...

DONA PAULA
(faint smile)
I'm here every evening, especially on nights like these.

PAULO
Are you alone here? It looks like a pretty deserted
place for a woman to be by herself.

DONA PAULA
(smiles)
I'm usually up there...
She points to a Romanesque white structure glowing in the Full
Moon light, at the top of a rocky outcrop.

DONA PAULA (cont'd)
Looking down at couples, making promises to each other.
Some are kept.. some die out as the moons go by.

PAULO
Promises should never be broken.

DONA PAULA
But they are... On many a full moon night I see people
here throw rings, necklaces into the sea...
(LONG BEAT)
Mementos, of promises broken.

PAULO
That could explain why the moon shimmering
off the water looks...

PAULO   DONAPAULA
...like beads of pearls   ...like beads of pearls

She laughs, softly, with a kind of lilting warmth.

DONA PAULA (cont'd)
Except, on full moon nights like this, when it is.

PAULO
What is?

DONA PAULA
When it's really pearls shimmering out on the sea.

PAULO
Ahh...The lady of the sea, wearing a pearl necklace
looking for her lover? I've heard that story.

DONA PAULA
Is that why you came here tonight?

PAULO
Yeah, something about that folktale...

DONA PAULA
It's no folklore...see for yourself.

She points to the sea. We turn around and see the silhouette of a
shapely, translucent woman slowly rise from the water, her hair
in a roman braid, wearing only a glowing string of pearls. The
woman glides over the water... towards the jetty...passing by us,
merging into Dona Paula.

DONA PAULA (cont'd)
(behind us)
You said you'd be back in a day. It took you 400 years.

We see a glowing pearl necklace around Dona Paula's neck.
PAULO
D...Dona..Paula Amaral

(beat)
Antonio de Souto Maior...

DONA PAULA
(eyes welling up)
Promises are never broken... Paulo.

DONA PAULA (cont'd)
I knew you'd come back for me. I knew we'd be together, again.

She reaches out toward us as she fades away slowly... The string of pearls falls to the floor of the jetty and roll out to the sea.

FADE TO BLACK

Cinematic Storyboard And Scene Blocking:

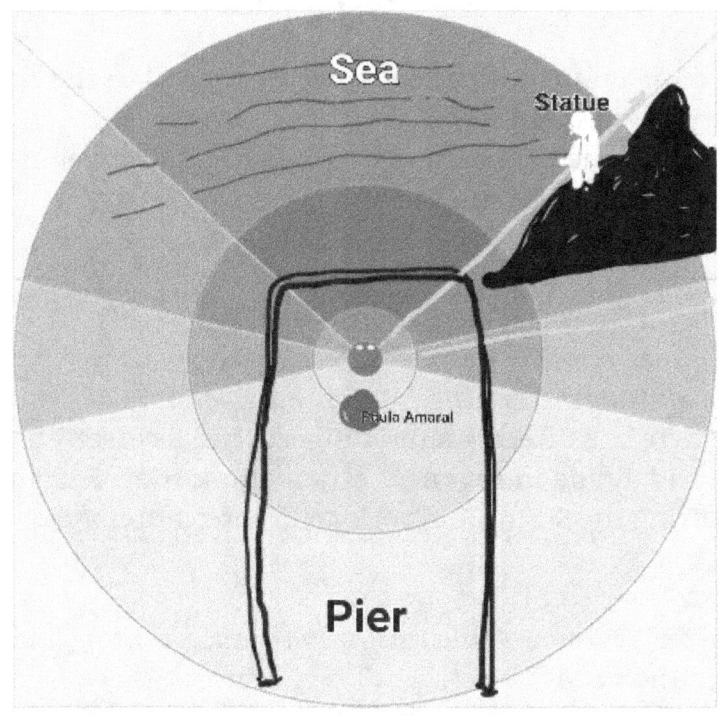

Storyboarding and scene blocking for Cinematic VR films can be done in many ways. The template I've used above comes from Vincent McCurley. The internet has some good templates one can readily download and they come in different layouts, including place for production info as well as "establishing shots." An acknowledged and popular method is to chart the whole 360° or 180 degree field of view in a diagram and then sketch in the opening "framing" and other elements in the scene.

Remember, the audience is free to look all around if inside a 360 VR video (or a realtime Game Engine created story-world). For VR 180° videos, the field of view is baked-in to cover half the field of view.

Breaking down the Script...

"...The night is setting in as the last few couples leave
the pier. We stand by the edge of the rail looking out
at sea..."
The screen play gives us a few clues here to plan the scene. We know certain things:
1) We can assume this VR movie needs full 360 coverage as we'll see people walking past us and away.
2) This shot will be in first person POV

...FADE OUT/IN
Still on the pier, our POV opens to a rocky outcrop with
a distinct whitewashed statue... we hear..."
This is where the Director subtly hijacks the Headset View with a fade out and a fade in to a new establishing shot. Reframing the scene to bring the Statue and rocky cliff into center view.

"...CUT TO:
Third person POV show Paulo raising his head, squinting and lifting a
pair of binoculars to his eyes..."
It's the first time we get to see Paulo. Can you guess where the VR camera would be? That's right, we'd need to move it a few feet away from the rail and edge of the Pier where it was for the

previous shot. This is so that we respect the 'spatiality' of the scene. Since it's shot in stereoscopic 3D, we can judge distance rather accurately, and wouldn't want the camera to be "breathing down" (how close we the audience are to the actor) Paulo's neck. We need to respect and maintain personal space, just as in real life.

"...CUT TO:
POV of Binocular masking, looking at statue..."
How do we 'force' focus in a 360 movie? One way is to employ devices such as a Binoculars-effect mask. Now this cannot be done every time and has to be motivated. Here, the motivation is, he's looking at a faraway statue. We do have other tools such as lighting and positional audio. The previous 3rd person POV which showed Paulo craning his neck and squinting as well as the 'Cut' to (reframe to) the statue are examples of forced focus or, a "headset hijack" being executed by the Director. If this were a 180 VR film, things would be a lot easier and akin to conventional 2D filmmaking.

Dona Paula - An Extended Reality Film:
The AR (Augmented reality) extension for the film could go something like this: For the next 50 years, on every full moon night, the app that contains the film, turns on your phone's camera [or Mixed Reality eyewear's cameras] and the user "sees" Dona Paula standing in front of you wearing a pearl necklace saying the end lines. As this could also be a Location Based AR film...if you are at the actual geo coordinates (Dona Paula jetty) on a full moon night, you'd see her rise from the water and glide toward the pier/jetty.

Exercise: If this were a completely CGI VR film authored in a Game Engine how would the Cinematography be? Note: if the pier was an actual 3D photogrammetry scan of the location, and then further optimized to run in VR, or indeed, in Mixed Reality, this would afford the audience, 6Dof to move around the Pier and Dona Paula herself. There are time sequencing methods to accomplish storytelling in the two popular game engines; Unity as well as Unreal Engine. *Cutscene,* is the terminology to search for!

The partial script-breakdown on the previous pages are to seed ideas for immersive Storytellers. Rules have not yet been written. There are no gurus. It's up to you to define the path forward in evolving the art from Storytelling to Storyliving!

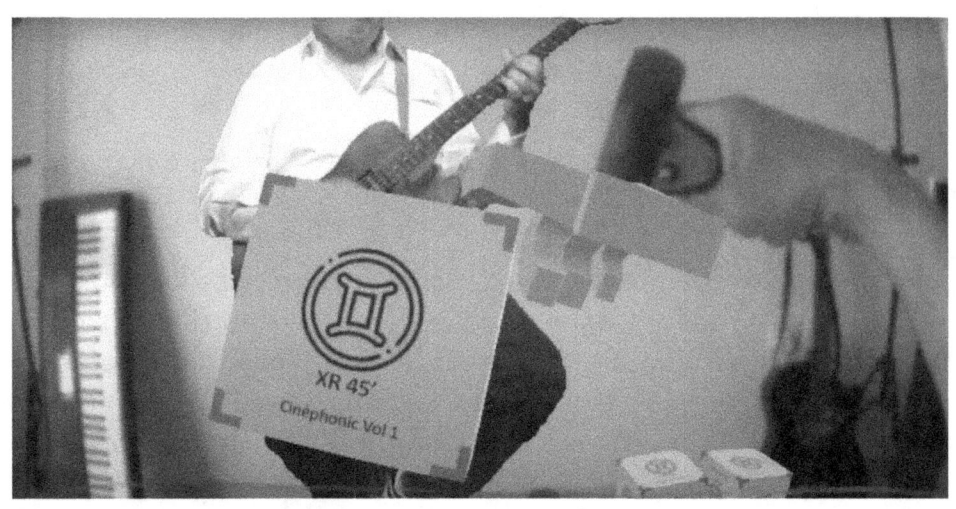

RP45'S: IMMERSIVE MUSIC STORYTELLING

E very song we hear is a "story" told in 5 minutes or thereabouts and it's satisfying, don't you agree? I feel the Music Industry is ripe for disruption...and the time is now!

So what's an RP45? We've had 45's, LPs and EPs. [Terminology in the music industry, describing length and number of songs pressed on vinyl records.] The music industry now enters an era of Reality-Play records; 4 to 5 minutes an immersive 'record', with 4 to 5 *stories* per RP album...In coining RP45's - it's my tribute to the era and nostalgia of vinyl records. Other reasons are explained below:

- An explosion in demand of Immersive Music is slated.

At least one major Mixed Reality maker is speaking about immersive audio.

- There's not been much innovation in the Music industry since the Napster streaming days.

The ability to 'experience' music, rather than passively hear or watch music (videos), appeals to all, from Generation Y to Gen Alpha. Every song is a "Story." Gen Z & Alpha might prefer an avatar flavor... Me? I'd lean toward an "unplugged" version of my fave artiste, while relaxing in a couch, either streaming an album via my favorite music streaming app, in immersive audio (more below) or soon, wearing eye-wear from one or the other Big-VR players, and *inviting the artiste* into my living space.

Imagine the late Whitney Houston in your living room, sitting across you, with a soulful rendition of "Saving all my Love for you" in immersive audio...or one of today's idols doing similar.

Cinéphonic: RP45's

...is what I'm keen to produce and I'm hoping you as immersive Storytellers feel the same after this conversation. The first RP45 album could perhaps feature 5 artistes, re-working acoustic / unplugged versions of their songs, and re-mastering in a Universal immersive sound format. Everything could run from standard web infrastructure, compatible with all streaming and OTT platforms as well as over mobiles. Most immersive headset manufacturers have stated they will support 'WebXR' that makes cross-platform universal Mixed Reality...a reality. The header image of this chapter shows a Mixed Reality / AR RP45 experienced from a standard web server via WebXR.

Discovering an Open Source Surround Audio Format:
The discovery: EAR. Thanks to BBC R&D and others, this OS and codec-agnostic format for next generation audio even uses

one of the most cost effective, yet powerful DAWs [digital audio workstations] out there. The best part; it's free! It also makes the format ideal to explode to other immersive audio authoring formats (Cinema, Home Theaters), should there be a need to release a recording that needs dedicated speaker arrays.

If you are considering dipping your toes in immersive entertainment (and you are, since you're reading this book) you should reach out to Music labels, indie Singers/Artists and encourage them to check out this new format of Immersive Music.

Advice for Headset & Eyewear Manufacturers:
Video-see thru is where it's at right now for Mixed Reality; proper stereoscopic video-seethru. Meta's Quest series of headsets does it right and is the gold standard for *stereoscopic video see-thru* mixed reality at an affordable cost. Apple's VR headset will certainly do it right with their imminent release in 2024. I have a feeling makers of some of the competing headsets don't have Creative Tech advisory on-board and they have some catch-up to do. Why have monoscopic passthru? The experience is flat. It does no justice to the experience of watching artistes in spatial 3D in mixed reality. The difference is night and day as far as true immersion goes.

When I first saw the music video for the Guns 'n Roses song 'November Rain,' it was nothing short of inspirational. An Oscar winning short film contender! was my first impression. Cinematic XR excels as an immersive entertainment medium for short films. Why not pioneer via music video storytelling. Your thoughts?

PART 4 - THE CINEMATIC METAVERSE

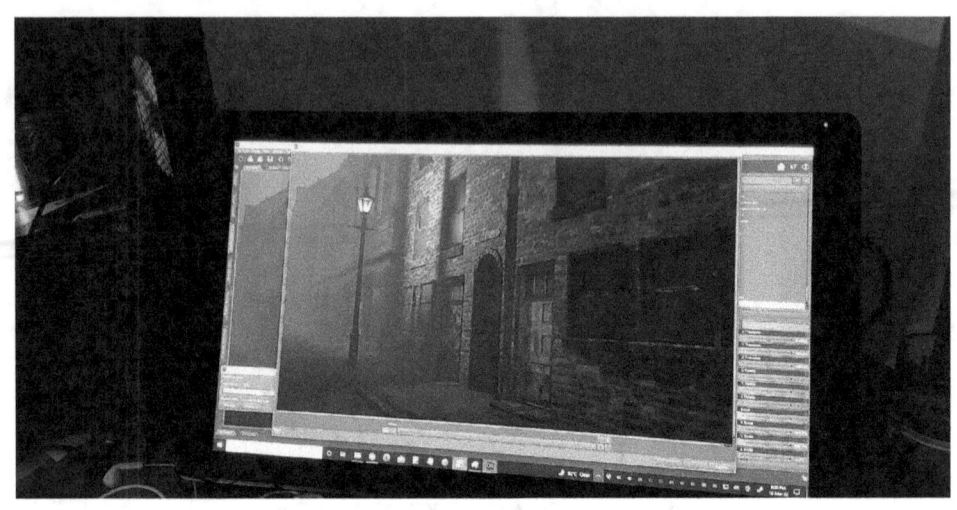

STORY LIVING IN THE XR METAVERSE?

If I 'meet' with my UK based producer in Whitechapel, old London, and we discuss set dressing and actor blocking for an XR production of Jack The Ripper, while I sit in Dubai wearing a VR headset and we speak in our own voices the way gamers do, does it qualify as "work" in the Metaverse?

More importantly; that a Metaverse (miniverse?) actually existed...even if for the duration of one project? What if this miniverse seeded a more persistent, city block scaled, 1888 digital overlay over London's Whitechapel Road, where one enters and explores, donning a Mixed Reality headset...while bumping into GPT driven A.I. 'Mary Jane Kelly' from Jack the Ripper's world?

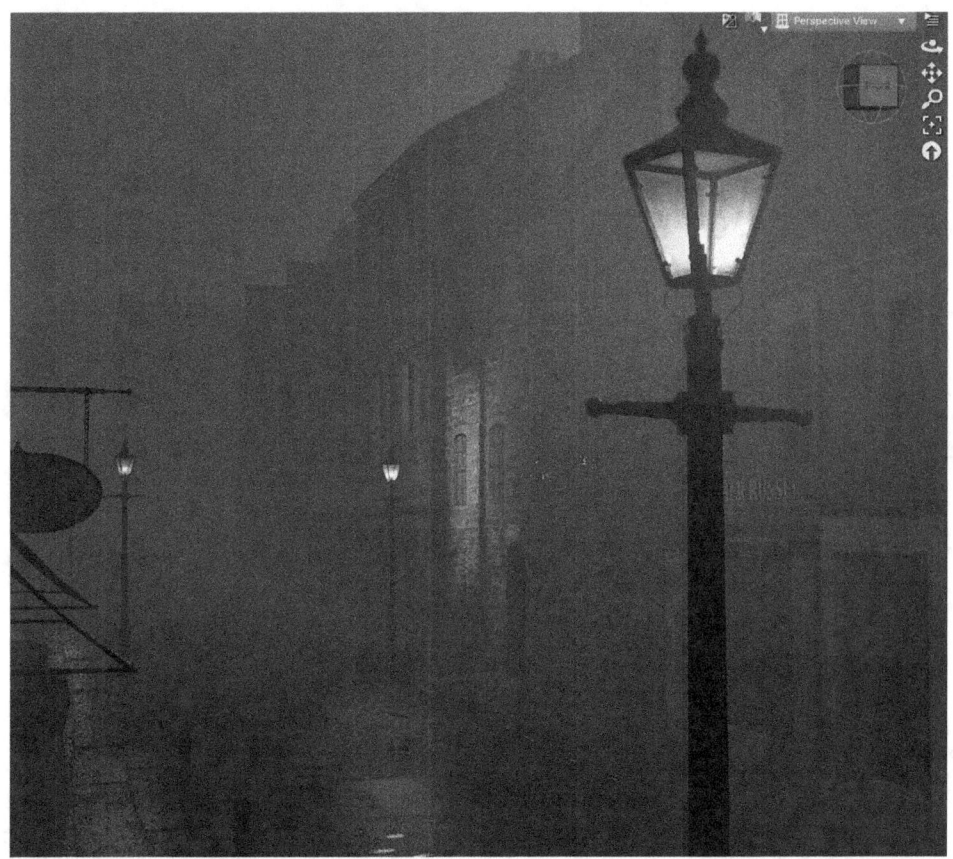

As Filmmakers, we need to gear up and evolve our craft from Storytelling to StoryLiving.

...In the coming decade I predict steampunk style low profile video-see thru headsets giving us a choice to live in this alternate Victorian world while we walk our real world. Would this then qualify as living in the Metaverse?

Two thoughts emerge from these musings:

1) The VR-only flavor of the Metaverse can be used perfectly well as a spatial visualization and collaboration tool in its current incarnation.

2) The 'everyday Metaverse'; to satiate our primitive brain's desire for visual authentication and human-to- human closeness, will be an XRMetaverse, experienced via video see-thru 'steam-punk profile goggles' that can be de-polarized if visual access to the analog world is needed.

Just as today I cannot compose an email without donning a visual aid -a pair of 18th century invented "eyewear" called spectacles, which brings me clarity of vision to function, so will there be a need in the coming decade of good form-factor headsets or eye-wear that the emerging generation will readily use (out of choice) to navigate their world of infotainment.

That emerging generation, I call GENXR. More about them (as our audiences) in the next chapter.

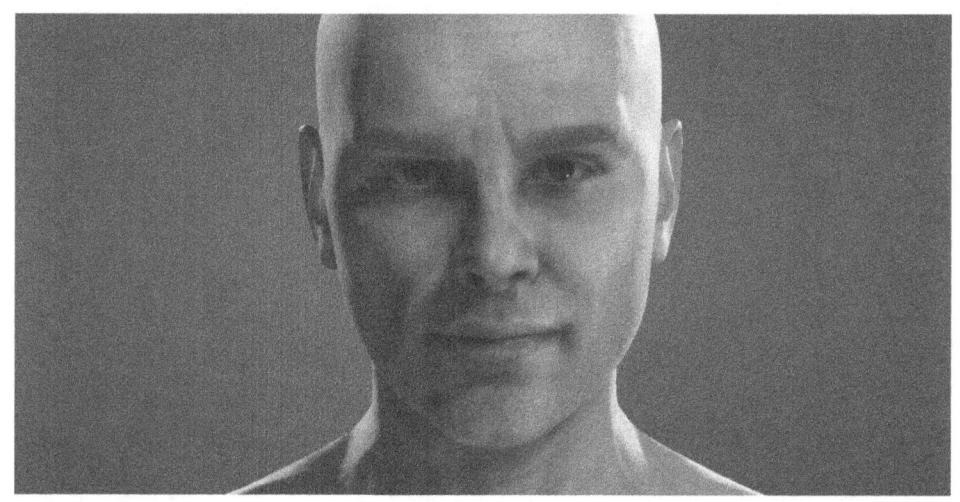

VIRTUAL HUMANS IN
THE METAVERSE

There's no way I look anything like my virtual self. When I'm "him" I can sing and perform on stage & it's obvious I won't ever age. I can change skin tone on-demand, but I prefer to walk in the Metaverse in human-like form (while mingling comfortably with cat/horse face avatars.)

I'd love to meet a casting agent in the Cinematic Metaverse. Perhaps on the sets of a movie being shot in the Metaverse itself. As we saw in the previous chapter -I could be strolling down the streets of 1888 London and bump into a talent scout. Yet, some of my fears are: What happens if one of the Metaverses doesn't acknowledge my Virtual self? What if they "De-rezz" me into a blocky mess if I enter a Cryptoverse? I had a bad dream the other night, seeing girl-bunnies in one of them cryptoverses with pixelated err..bits 'n bobs. Not a nice dream, that. What about identity theft? What if someone steals my identity and the next thing I know, I'm seen in the "wrong metaverse" doing unmentionable things.

What about the XRMetaverse? you know...the world scale Augmented Metaverses that organizations such as SnapChat or Niantic or TikTok might give birth to? Maybe even Google with its GeoSpatial OS? When I'm walking IRL (in real life) in my digital skin, sporting a virtual 6 pack overlaid on my meatbag body...I fear people in other metaverses will see hints of a beer belly and gray hair as I walk the real world, 'cause most of the Open Metaverse might not be compatible with some wall gardened metaverses? What accessories will I wear - NFT sneakers? Sounds good - but what if I enter a Metaverse running on some blockchain that's not compatible with another...will my expensive NFT sneakers follow through? Oh, I hope they will!

Wait! What's this rambling got to do with Cinematic Filmmaking in the Metaverse? Let's see... We've seen in the previous chapter, how movies might have real-world set extensions that audience can "live" in; can visit, in real life. There'll soon be a time where people living in London, could choose to either stroll in their boring "today world" or visit the evolving "story world" of Jack the Ripper's 1888 White Chapel.

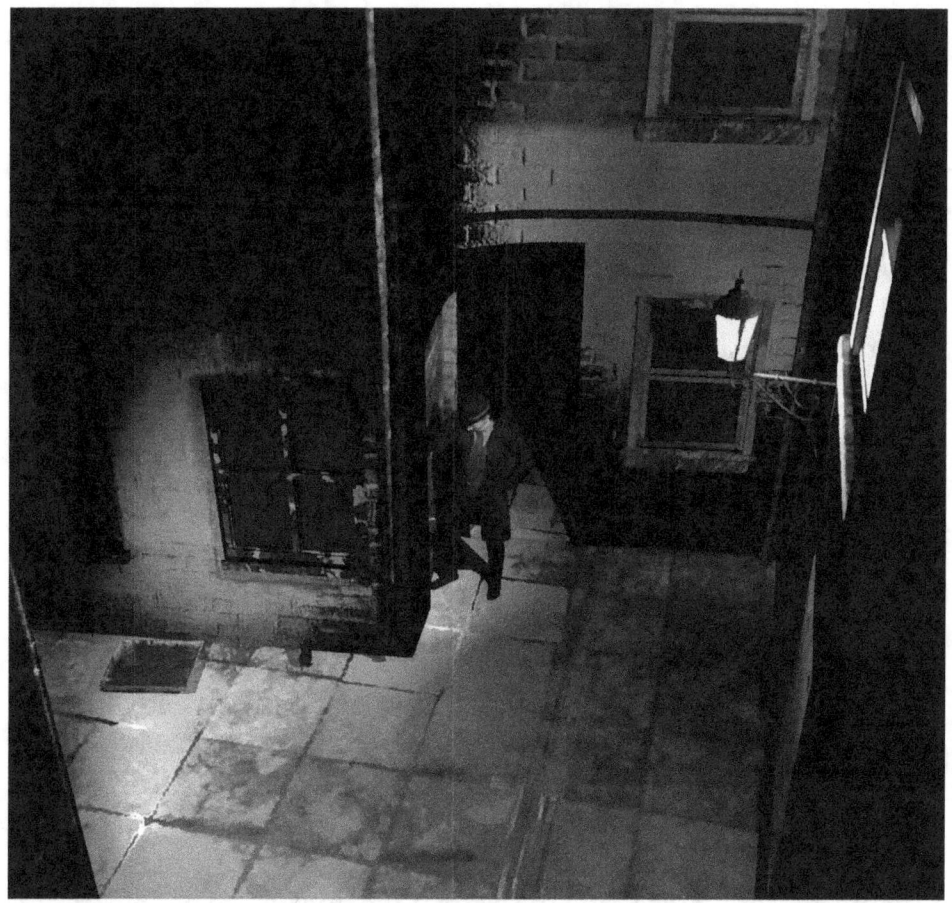

GenXR and Cult Entertainment:

Dateline - 1888, Millers Court, Dorset Street, London: Dorset street does not exist in today's London like it used to back in 1888 and there is no Miller's Court anymore. But it certainly can in the XR Metaverse. A movie studio might invest in genre IP (Intellectual Property) like Jack the Ripper, complete with an XR metaverse overlay. The cult of the Ripper has a fascinating following, worldwide. What if GenXR get hooked on this fascinating cult?

Who Is Genxr?

We must remember today's generation is at ease with identifying themselves as gender neutral, as they are, repping themselves in digital worlds via bespoke Avatars. Entertainment is already shifting to 'metaverses'...no, this isn't sci-fi; there's already been 'concerts' held in online game worlds (which are metaverses) hosting crowds of 12 million people as avatars. This generation - the GenXR will be tomorrow's 'movie audiences.' As storytellers we'll need to extend the narrative from the over a century old silver screen, to the Cinematic Metaverse.

The Cult Of The Ripper:

The Cult of Ripper audiences will either be online in a VR flavor of the Ripper Metaverse; a faithful recreation of Dorset street and Miller's Court where that fateful day, Mary Kelly was murdered...or, they might actually visit the location in real life, and see the facade of old 1888 Dorset street overlaid at the very same location. While structures get demolished and the old makes way for the new...I am told, at least in 2012, and it might even hold true today, there's still a gap in the curbstones on the pavement where the archway entrance to Miller's Court (Mary Kelly's residence) stood. Imagine hundreds of such Cinematic Metaverses, tied in to story-worlds where people (fans?) congregate to discuss *your stories*, either via VR metaverses or the XR Metaverse. That! is the future of storyliving and as a filmmaker or storyteller, is what we should gear up for.

Virtual Actors in your living room? Check the chapter on OTT in the Metaverse. It promises to provide some food for thought!

I'll go now...this meat bag needs to rest. I'll let my virtual human self; my Dirrogate [Digital Surrogate] take over, powered by the latest iteration of a GPT and LLM artificial intelligence...just as the characters of Jack, Mary Kelly, Joseph Barnett...will carry out their virtual lives in the Ripper Metaverse.

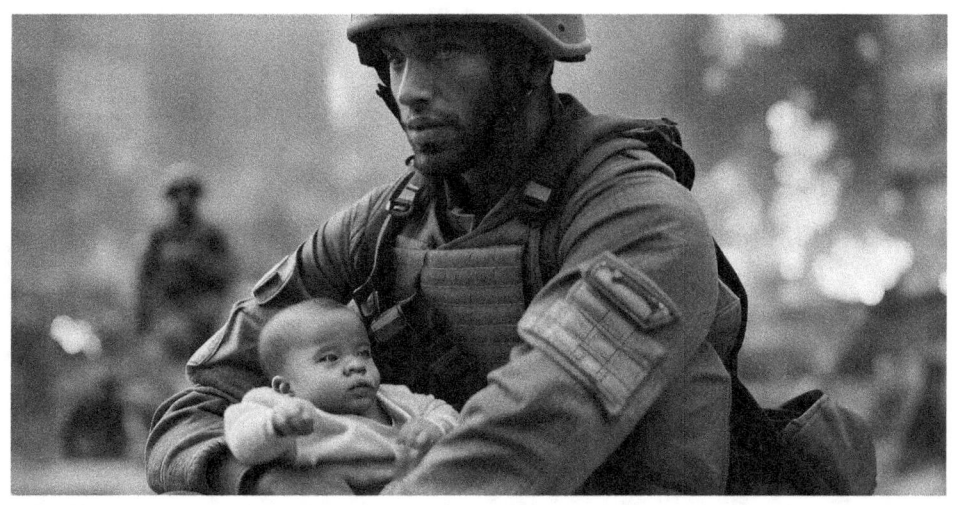

FACTUAL STORYTELLING & IMMERSIVE JOURNALISM

5 years ago, I travelled to Mumbai, landing right as the 'monsoon' season kicked in. The plan: To immerse (pun unintended) audiences in NEWS and factual storytelling, in Virtual and Augmented reality.

I spent the next 7 months with one of the bigger NEWS agencies, helping them develop an immersive journalism Dept. An interesting all-weather VR camera was created along with training of field reporters in best practices on filing video based VR NEWS snippets that could be accessed by audiences through the Newspaper's online portal.

Now, some years later, the Metaverse affords us an opportunity to "collectively" be immersed in a virtual space, to *re-live and discuss* NEWS-worthy events that played out in the past, or in-situ, via newer tech advances such as Nvidia's Instant NeRF, allowing us to experience and explore snapshots of time.

News in The Metaverse - Will it affect us emotionally?

In the year 2015, I was reading about NYTVR [https:// tinyurl.com/NYTVRAR] It was nothing short of euphoric! They were bringing the world -the real world- closer to all of us through Virtual Reality. Almost 10 year later during a lecture on Immersive Journalism, it got me thinking: The NEWS in the Metaverse —would it affect us emotionally? After all, if the Metaverse affords for full immersion, either as we enter it donning Virtual Reality eyewear or, if the Metaverse gets "pulled" into our world via Augmented Reality; I call it the XRMetaverse...would we then be "living the NEWS"; experiencing factual stories play out around us?

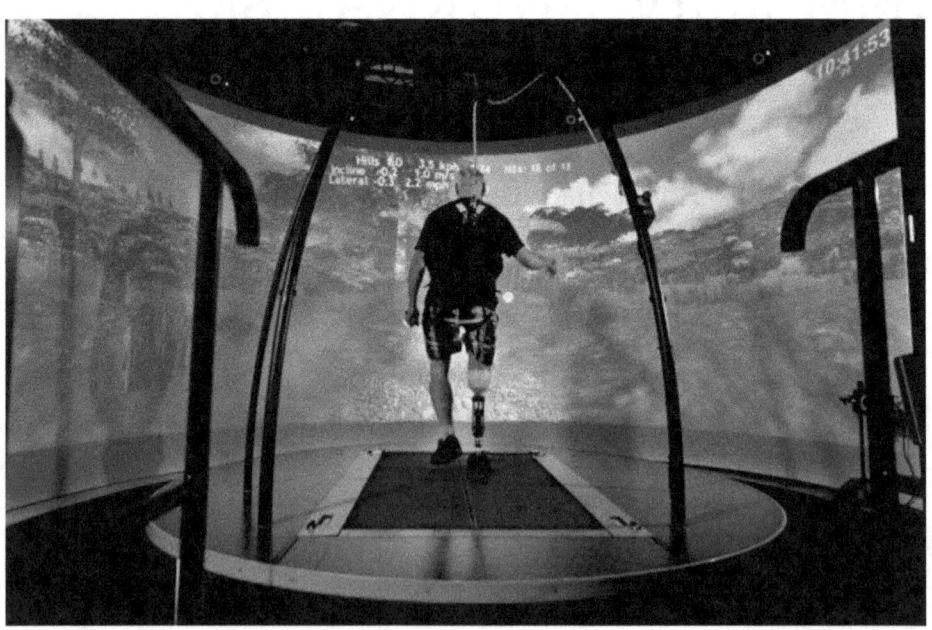

The answer is simple –A Simulation of a real life scenario is the next best thing to actually being there. CAREN [https://www.motekmedical.com/solution/caren/] is being used to help deal with PTSD, and other associated psychological and physiological battle scars, as is the Brave Mind system. [https://tinyurl.com/skiprizzo] Systems similar to BraveMind, are now affordable (via current VR HMDs and computers) and within reach for treatment of patients suffering from a multitude of such ailments. We now know via these systems, how the Virtual world can affect and influence our Reality.

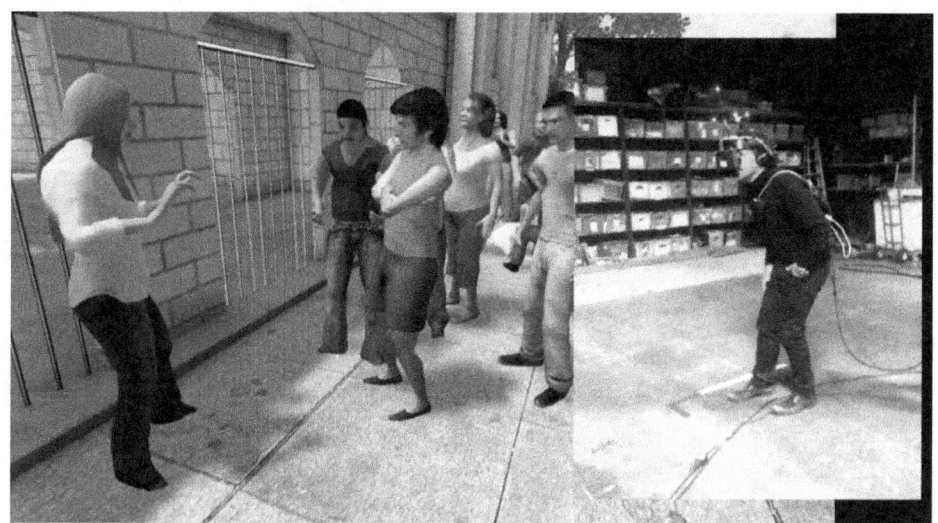

Story Living in the Metaverse:
"Hunger in Los Angeles" [https://tinyurl.com/hungerLA] is a recreation of a real life event. Being immersed in the scene wearing VR headwear, does have an effect on the viewer of this NEWS story. Imagine what might happen if this were the aftermath of a man-made disaster or natural calamity and we were "living it" as a re-creation in the Metaverse discussing it in own voices with other metaverse visitors, some from the next town, others, from half way across the world. Would it trigger a heightened sense of collective empathy?

It is worth arguing that the NEWS, if presented in an immersive environment, might then: Galvanize us into action? —As passive consumers of the NEWS, we have quickly become desensitized to human suffering, but just as soldiers are being immersed in VR, maybe the realism of NEWS stories recreated in the Metaverse, could move us into positive action against the plague of war? Or, make us push the Donate button, when we're "standing" right there in the middle of a synthetic world, seeing, perhaps on a subconscious level, even 'feeling' the suffering of refugees or famine.

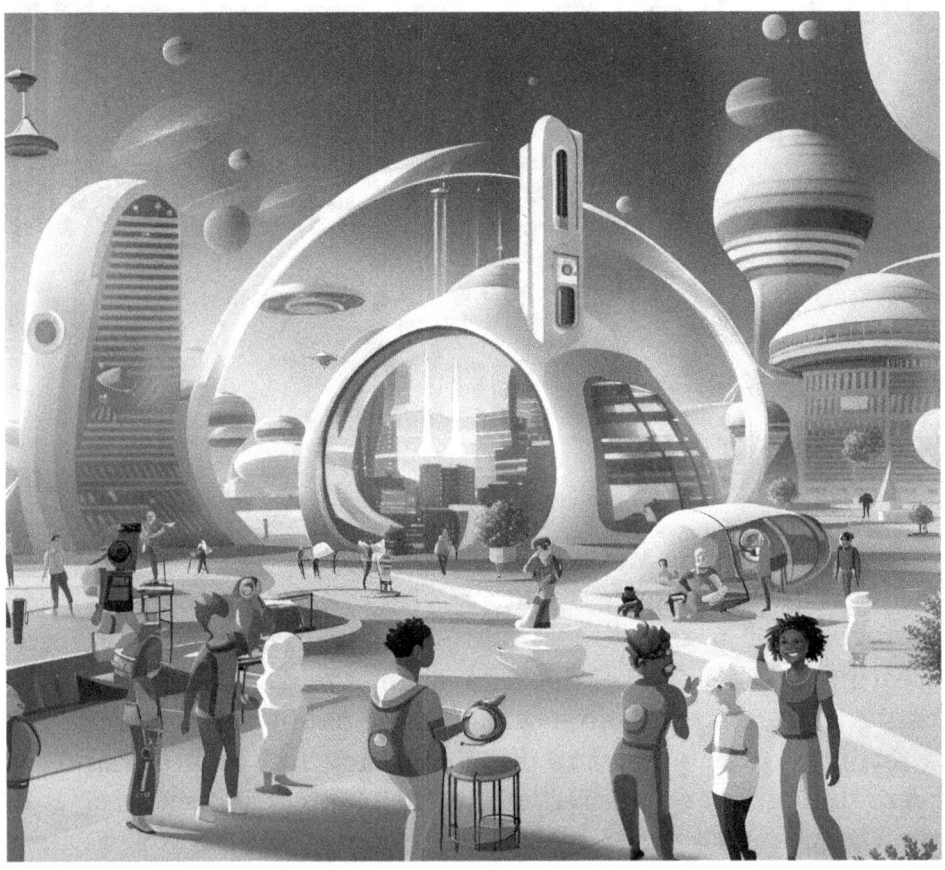

The Social Metaverse:

NEWS in the Metaverse does not have to be all about suffering. Sports NEWS, the Red Carpet at the Oscars and other feel good moments can also relieve stress from a hectic day at work. People can come home and choose to jump into the Metaverse to escape the drudgery of their everyday reality. Sporting events as far back as the 2014 FIFA Soccer World-Cup brought the realism of having Goal side seats and perimeter-like first-hand realism when viewed by audiences in 3D Cinemas in many countries. With Virtual Reality eye-wear now in millions of homes, will sports "miniverses" complete with commentators, be a place where people tele-port to and congregate?

The Cinematic Metaverse:
The big Metaverse companies offering full immersion with their VR hardware and social platforms already allow for the viewing of movies in a grand cinema like environment. Will the Cinematic Metaverse be the final nail in the coffin of the brick 'n mortar Silver screen?

MBO (Meta Box Office?) could be a new house-hold acronym. It's not hard to see the couple of first mover organizations who've successfully launched their video see-thru Mixed Reality Headsets, monetizing *their* flavor of the Metaverse with access to live events and entertainment, while allowing seamless engagement with friends and family or making new friends across the world.

FOOD FOR THOUGHT: TOWARDS A CINEMATIC METAVERSE 2.0

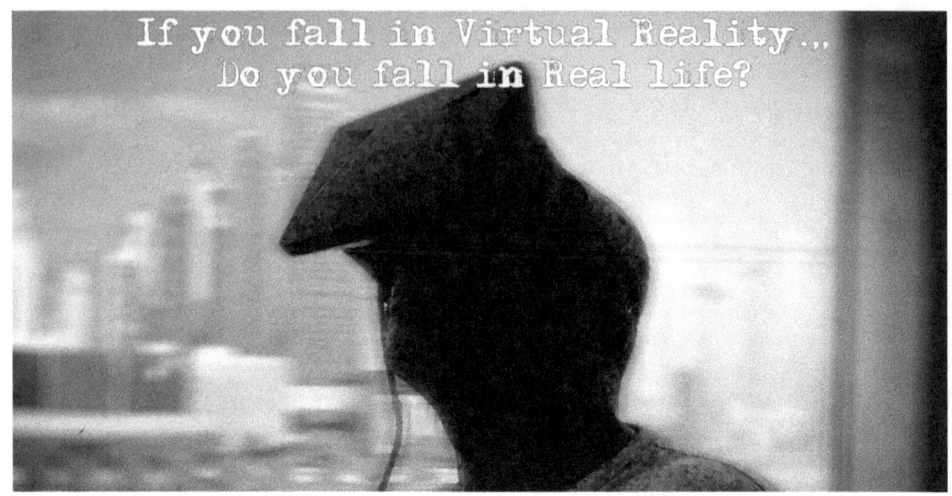

If you fall in Virtual Reality...
Do you fall in Real life?

WHY METAVERSE 1.0 FAILED.

Hardly a month went by, between the years 2021 and 2022, without an overdose of YAM (yet another metaverse) Everyone wanted in, from Real Estate companies, to Retailers...to government Depts. —all rushing in, fueled by Venture Capital who later slowly began realizing their folly by not doing due diligence on the many startups they were throwing millions($) at. Sounds familiar? It should. That's what the dot com boom felt like a few decades earlier...well, we know how that played out.

Yet, as those who've been around since the first iteration of Bubblenomics know, the race to build metaverses came with a strong sense of de-ja vu. What could have been done differently? Here's three areas that should (could?) be rectified to set things right:

Metaverse: NTFs & Crypto or a Higher Calling?

Almost every pitch deck to Venture Capital firms had to have Crypto, Block Chain or NFTs, or all three mashed together to gain investor interest. From healthcare startups (perhaps they thought encoding human DNA on the blockchain had merit?)...to digitizing grandma's cross-stitch patterns and selling it as "pixel art" while touting scarcity as the reason people would buy in. Not such a bad idea, if indeed it was grandma's real one-of-a-kind hand crafted labor. However, what was bringing in huge VC funding was pixel-art generated by algorithms and computer programs that were given instructions to alter a few pixels to make each "art piece," rare(!)

The Metaverse is so much more! The Metaverse is meant to build community and to facilitate the connection of minds to advance us as a species. *This,* is the higher calling of the Metaverse. If pitch-decks can prove they can ease communication and interaction in more immersive ways than what Web2.0 is offering, they are on the right track with their need for funding.

There are so-called metaverses already built and now languishing; as we'll see in the next two shortcomings; they were doomed from the get go.

World Building: Editing and Navigation

Navigation: The purpose of the Metaverse is immersion and interaction of a level beyond keyboard, mouse and touch-screen. In short, all the crypto-verses and even some of the non crypto flavored metaverses that launched, prioritized desktop or phone based gateways to the metaverse, and they failed, miserably. Immersion via a 7 inch cellphone screen can only go so far. While it's good for watching OTT content and two of the largest populations on the planet consume content on these devices this way, there is still a higher level of immersion needed, and is a reason for Metaverse1.0 's failure.

It's my opinion that we need to revisit VR cellphone holders; "Metaverse spectacles," so we can see better at the scale we should, for immersion to happen. Samsung's GearVR was great when it first came out and needs to be resurrected, perhaps a light-weight foldable 2.0 version with glass lenses. Cellphones already have processing power built in.

For example: I prefer watching a Netflix movie in one of the outdated cellphone VR holders, than I do on a VR headset that I'm lugging around at airports. The cellphone just slips right out of the holder for use for the better part of the day.

These areas of design need to be addressed on a war footing and funded by Venture Capital, rather than the next "evaluated at over 2 billion" startup with yet another NFT idea.

Avatar Interoperability:

Or...the Emperor's new clothes and NFTs. Between 2020 - 2022, it was a free-for-all reign in that department, thanks in part to bored apes, pimped out hippos, crypto kittens and a myriad other expensive crypto-avatars floating around looking for Metaverse dominance, vying for a person's crypto currency in an attempt to allow people to 'express their individuality' [expensively] in the Metaverse. Yet, imagine one's embarrassment when entering non-compatible cryptoverses running on competing 'blockchains,' only to be seen stark *naked* because, well, one's avatar "skin" was not recognized by the gatekeepers running that particular ~~metaverse~~ cryptoverse.

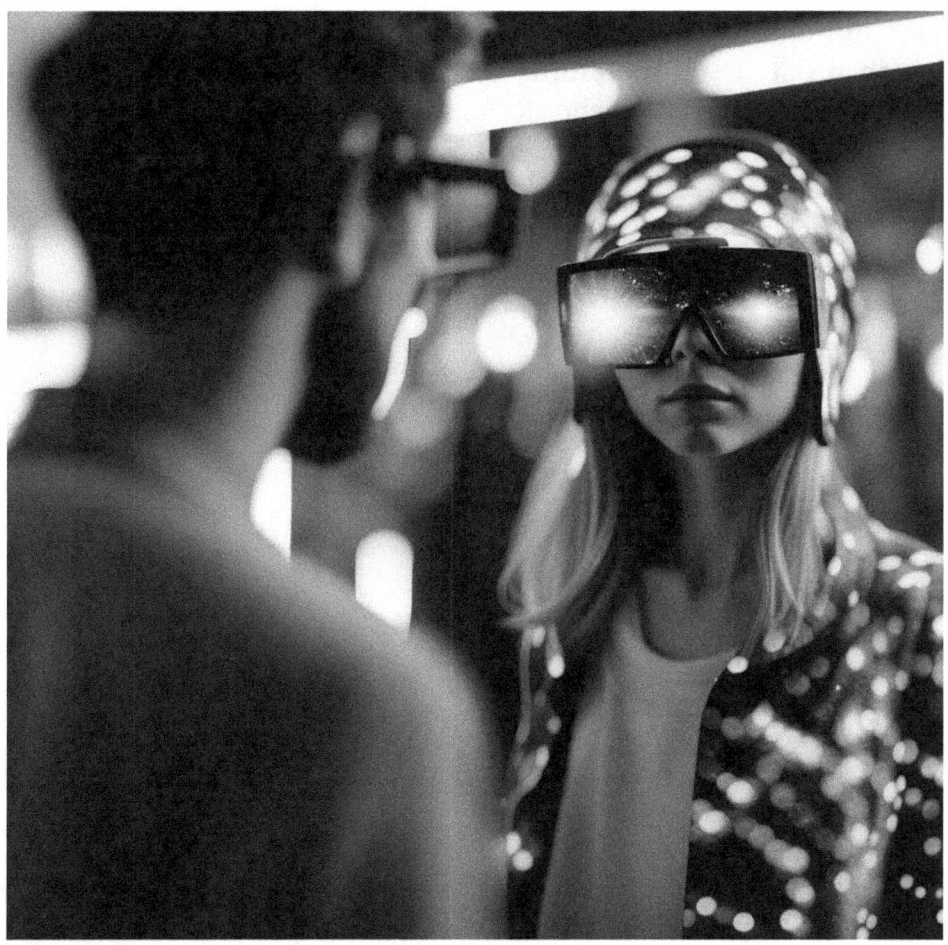

Oh yes -- the Metaverse will spill out into the real world. That's the whole point of it. GenXR will choose to walk in the real world, while interacting with digital twins of their friends, seen in-situ, augmenting their world-space. The *world* you walk on/ in, could be the planet Earth, the Moon or Mars - Metaverse to Multiverse, you see.

How are new startups planning on addressing the stumbling blocks of Metaverse 1.0, to create smooth customer experiences and make meaning in the Metaverse? These are questions that Venture Capitalists should be made to ask and possibly held accountable for (by their investors) when funding startups with inflated multi- billion dollar evaluations...These are also questions storytellers should be asking, as we contribute to the development of a better, more wholesome Metaverse 2.0.

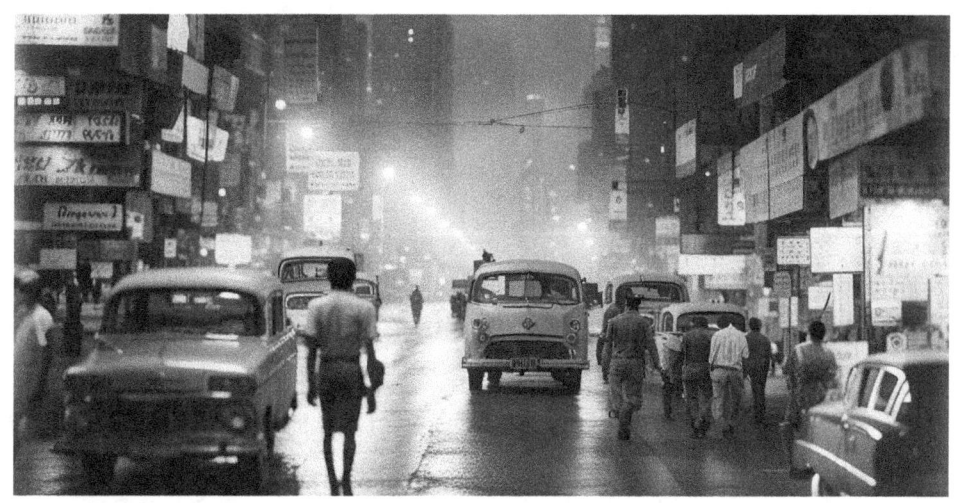

BANDRA WEST IS EVERYWHERE: THE SCARCITY FALLACY

B andra west, IRL (in real life) is home to Bollywood's mega stars. In an otherwise over crowded metropolis that is Mumbai, this suburb maintains its quaintness with colonial era cottages, greenery and a mix of accessible nightlife venues against a backdrop of skyscrapers, making it a highly desirable location.

The same holds for other mega cities; Clarke Quay in Singapore... Sh.Zayed Road, Dubai... Sunset Strip... However, unlike real life, where natural land formations, weather and economic activity dictate the price of property and where slums jostle for space with high-rises as the header picture exemplifies in the

Metaverse* many of these constraints do not hold water (a little foreshadowing there).

Myth: LAND SCARCITY IN THE METAVERSE: Scarcity in the Metaverse, is a myth. A myth propagated by unscrupulous crypto brokers - whose sole motivation is to speculate on profits of funny- money, a.k.a. cryptocurrency *after* a deal has been transacted. Thus their desire to turn the Metaverse into a 'Cryptoverse'. A world where every interaction is a Transaction.

They forget, for scarcity to work in virtual real-estate, one needs to abolish that ancient practice of...Teleporting

No one walks in the Metaverse. The mode of commuting is usually a laser point and click mechanic, to cover any amount of distance in a second. No downtown traffic to negotiate, no crowded footpaths to traverse. The Cryptoverses selling digital land parcels would have you believe that the same conditions that dictate prices IRL, apply to the Metaverse. Again, teleporting disproves it. The ability to spin up another server, disproves it. The premise of 'virtual society' as an argument does not hold true. In real life, yes, I'd likely not want to commute to 'Sobo' (South Bombay) to mingle, because it would take an hour. In the Metaverse I could mingle in virtual Times Square NY, and then teleport to Clarke Quay, Singapore, in a second. That's what the metaverse offers.

Plot Twist: THE XR METAVERSE

Who owns Bandra West in the XR Metaverse? - The Government, The Telcos, The Roads and Transport Authority? That's the right question to ask.

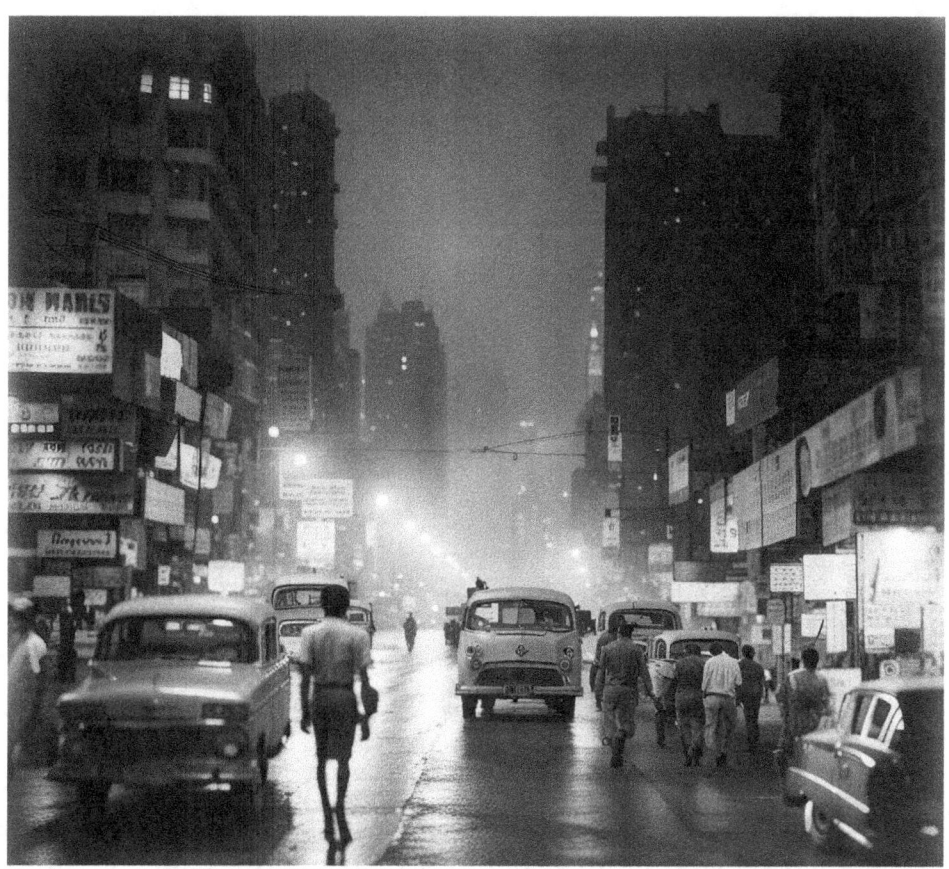

So far we've been looking at the Metaverse to be a virtual world that's either entered into typically via a VR headset for maximum immersion, or, accessed through a desktop computer or tablet. However, the XR- Metaverse can drape itself as a digital overlay -pin registered- to the real world, and seen via Mixed Reality eyewear, or today, via a cellphone camera; dubbed video-seethru AR. Solutions such as Google's Spatial API can make this happen. In hard sci-fi writings I'd asked in 2010; Will Google create a Surrogate Reality World? [https://tinyurl.com/googlesurrogate] Yet today, we can already experience it. So what does that mean for virtual real estate in the XR Metaverse? Surely, its value will proportionately skyrocket in tandem with its real world twin. Or will it?

Cryptoverse operators who currently sell "land" at ridiculous prices could even try to justify their shenanigans by saying their Metaverse is pin-registered to the real world where real world inhabitants will be populating it (either in person or as digital avatars of themselves) The problem is the metaverse needs to be accessed via a gateway -usually, a Telco gateway or portal.

Land Scarcity Fallacy: Part 2. Who Owns Real Estate In The Xr Metaverse

While 'crypto-influencers' sell the concept of "scarcity" in the Metaverse; a grift in my opinion…what does it mean to explore the XR Metaverse where Digital content is pin-registered to the real world? Surely then, the cryptoverse scarcity augment holds right? Or does it…

The argument made is that you want to buy land in the metaverse because it's going to be scarce and that a community is going to be built around there so you need to get in, fast. But, who travels by walking in the metaverse. No one travels by walking in the metaverse. If I know there's something fun happening in some part of this virtual universe, I'll teleport in there. I won't walk. The rules of physics and natural geography that govern navigation and transportation in the real world, do not apply.

> *Why is this important to Storytelling in the Cinematic Metaverse? Because; location, location, location! [but only for film tourism]*

The Xr Metaverse Explained:

Bukit Bintang, is a famous location in Kuala Lumpur Malaysia. Similarly, in Dubai, Sheikh Zayed road is prime real estate. Who owns these places in the Metaverse? As a storyteller, if I'm building a whole story-world in one metaverse [let's say one run by the company Meta]...what do I mean first of all, by the XR metaverse? Let's have a look:

There's the regular flavor of the Metaverse; a place where you 'jack in' via Virtual Reality headsets and then there's the Augmented Reality Metaverse, where digital assets [3D buildings, furniture, avatars] that comprise a metaverse, are pin-registered spatially, to the real world; GPS co-ordinates and all, and usually at world-scale as a digital overlay draped over the real world. This is what I label: *The XR Metaverse.* Imagine Time's Square, New york or the header image from this chapter; a street in Mumbai, in the real world, and you decide you want to put an ancient or even a futuristic structure via Augmented Reality, permanently (persistent AR) locked down right there to some well-known building.

You could pin register a digital asset to the facade of a building, say, a futuristic animated digital arch for AceHamBurger. But what platform are you using to view this augmented digital overlay? If you're in Meta's metaverse you could possibly use a future iteration of Instagram or Horizon World, as the gateway. What happens to those who use Snapchat to tune into their XR Metaverse? So let's say some big Ad agency was now contracted by KingHamBurger to use Snapchat to put up a whole competing digital façade, pin registered to that very same real world building facade.

Hijacking Air Space in the XR Metaverse.

People using Snapchat at that location are looking at KingHamBurger branding through their eyewear, while people who are using Instagram will see AceHamBurger. It's like hijacking virtual real estate air-space. So, in the end who controls the XR Metaverse or these Metaverses (multiverses?) as Mixed Reality eyewear goes mainstream? Does Apple control it? Apple might decide to have their own ecosystem. What happens if Google decides to do its own Metaverse and for that matter, what happens if the Telcos decide on their own flavor of Metaverse? People access the internet through some Telco or Telecommunication network. Could the Ministry of Transportation in Malaysia control the 'AR airspace' around Bukit Bintang, proclaiming any digital overlays there, only be authorized by them?

Xr Storyverse In Bandra West:

The header image shows a contemporary fictional street in Mumbai. Of interest might be the old 60's automobiles in that image. Those cars *could be* AR models seen while walking the street in real life, wearing immersive eye-wear, soon. We already can today, via cellphone AR. There was a Bollywood movie, Bombay Velvet, which had a nice film noir vibe to it. Now imagine if the makers of that film decide to have an XR Storyverse that extends the narrative, to real life!

Audiences in real world Mumbai, could live in the storyverse of Bombay Velvet, in the year 2033, while watching (interacting with?) GPT and LLM driven A.I. characters carry on their fictional lives as depicted in the film. There would be Digital facades, street signs and automobiles of the 60's and 70's superimposed over the real world. A storyverse the size of a single street in Bandra West, or an entire block sized storyworld to traverse. Would audiences and fans need to physically be there? Of course not! They could 'teleport' in from anywhere in the world via VR and enter the Bombay Velvet metaverse!

As future aware filmmakers and storytellers, these seemingly far out scenarios are worth thinking about...the Metaverse and storytelling...it opens our minds and can actually drive real conversations in an incubator, in a think tank, while we seed ideas on how to navigate the real world that's increasingly being digitalized.

We do this through the stories we tell as animators, as game designers, as filmmakers. It could inspire regulatory bodies and governments to think ahead, before disasters occur. Hopefully, the Metaverse evolves into a place that can bring people and minds together, unlike the real world, which is only polarizing and pushing people apart. The Metaverse could be a parallel world where like-minded people congregate to chart our course as a species with higher purpose.

CONCLUSION: The Metaverse is a world of Abundance not of Scarcity. Scarcity, if at all, will be driven not by rarity of NFTs (another fallacy there) or "Land parcel" sales.

"... It could be Bandra west or anywhere...Liverpool or Rome...'cause the Metaverse is everywhere..." -- h/t The Beautiful South: Rotterdam

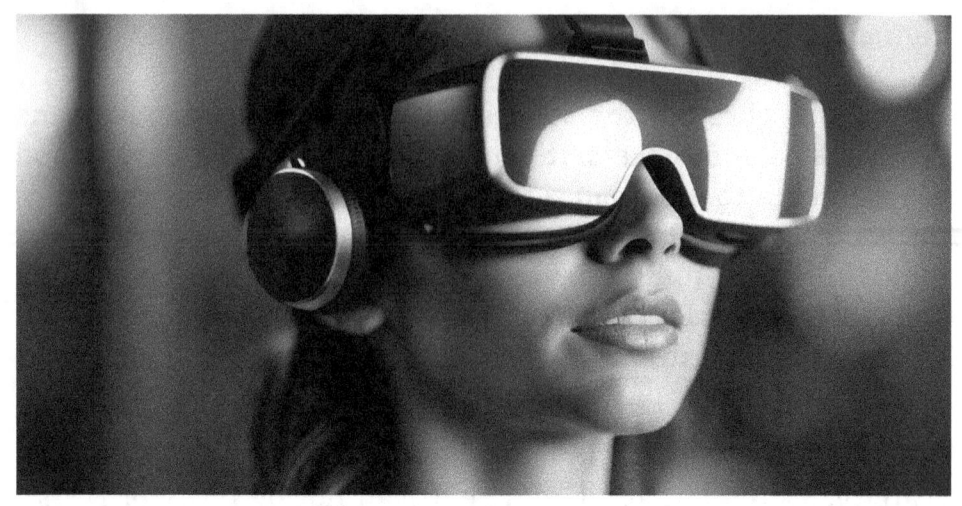

XR MOVIES IN THE OTT METAVERSE?

W hen travelling pre-pandemic; the Covid '19 one, one of the more relaxing experiences was sitting back in airport lounges, watching Netflix movie premieres on my own portable wide screen - The Oculus Quest headset.

I remember seeing the Netflix original, Bright, as well as numerous standup comedy shows as though sitting in my own private cinema. The effect is hard to describe; the nearest is imagining a home theater projection setup.

No 3D movies on OTT VR apps?
This brings up the question: Why aren't the OTT apps offering stereoscopic 3D versions of films when available? Granted, no one

talks about 3DTVs anymore, but finally there's a way to experience a story the way the film director intended, especially after Studios pay multimillion dollar fees to convert their blockbuster movies to 3D. OTT platforms are missing out!

XR Movies on OTT:

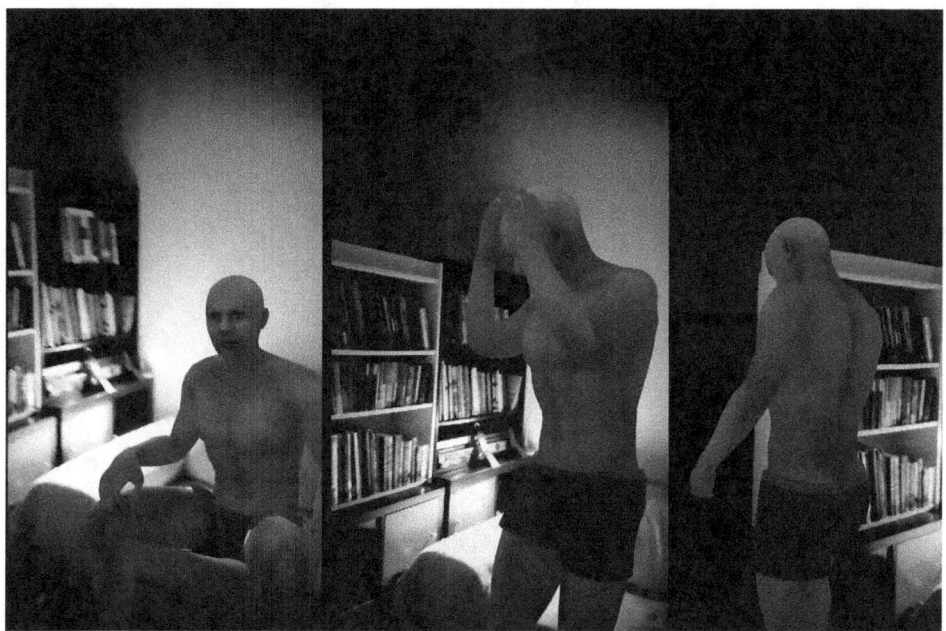

The film-strip shows a character stepping into *audience-space* in a scene depicting regret in a short Mixed Reality film I was experimenting with in early 2020. I'd first saw with immense fascination the possibilities of extending stories beyond the *proscenium* and invading audience's personal space, when I came across the brilliant "Fragments" on Microsoft's Hololens device. This was far ahead of the curve, compared to the abomination that was (is?) AR pew-pew alien shooters, or AR games featuring the collecting of fluffy AR CGI characters. AR is so much more than that, I kept saying. *Fragments,* was the game-changer.

Discovery of MARS:
Not the planet, but a powerful Augmented Reality authoring

system by the developers of the game engine, Unity. For the curious, it allows for spatial and semantic understanding of the real world (walls, floor, height of couches, dressers, tables...) An immersive storyteller can work with a Unity artist/coder to bring their imagination to life. The still images in the film strip shows the character walk into the audiences real world space, while the headsets passthru cameras simultaneously provide the visuals and input for scene understanding so the character can walk to a couch, sit down, hold his head in his hands and deliver his inner monologue. He then stands up...walks a few feet away from the audience and the scene fades away to black.

Imagine such Extended Reality short films, factual entertainment pieces, and even film extensions of mainstream movies being triggered directly through OTT apps that reside on headsets.

The Auto-Immersive OTT switch trick:
Many years ago, I was invited to the high tech campus headquarters of one of the leading autostereoscopic TV [no need for 3d glasses] manufacturers to discuss an autostereo content creation deal and offer advisory on software for content creation. They had a neat way of 'triggering' the TV to switch from regular 2D to Autostereo mode. The first scan-line of a video frame contained a particular pixel line wide color pattern that when read by the signal processing chip, triggered the TV to switch modes and play the scene in 3D. This methodology could be adapted by a playback app to trigger Mixed Reality headsets to turn on their pass-thru cameras and enter 'XR mode.'

Enter... YouTube in VR:
YouTube, as an OTT player & platform has been leagues ahead of others. From immersive audio (ambisonic) to the myriad of formats it supports. In 2019 I'd shot a Cinematic VR extension for a popular OTT episodic TV show. The episode was hosted on YouTube and afforded good immersion (3D 360 visuals and head

tracked audio) on most VR headsets.

The main immersive media companies; MAGS [bonus points for figuring out the companies in the acronym] should be having conversations with Storytellers and innovation artistes and not just engineers and marketing departments. On a positive note: The big two VR manufactures are already thought to be in full dive, building newer iterations of VR eye-wear and creating *their* Metaverses which will eventually become a way of life for GenXR. The website Shot on What has a list of over 200 titles of Hollywood / Bollywood movies that are either natively shot or converted 3D movies. This is a missed opportunity that Product Heads of OTT platforms should consider rectifying, asap.

With OTT merging with immersive eyewear, Cinematic XR storytelling might finally come of age.

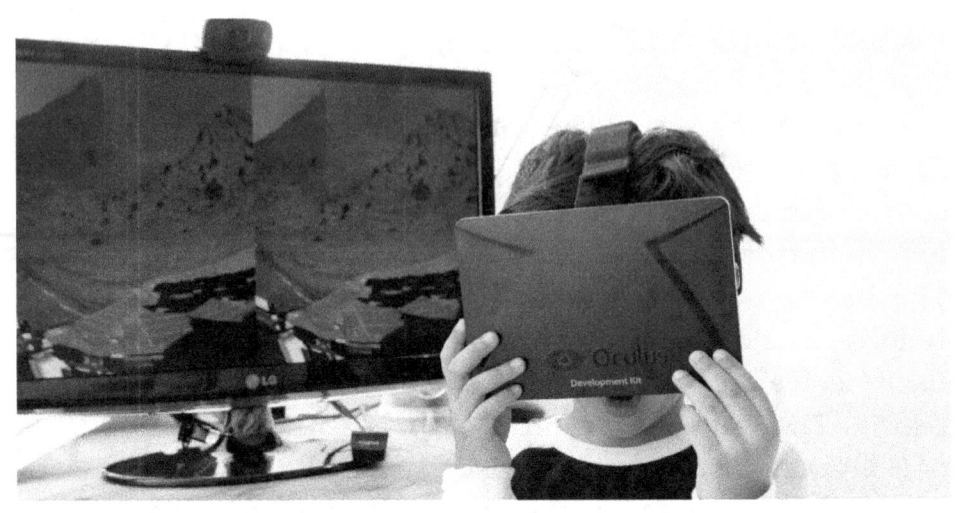

FIELD TRIPS IN CINEMATIC XR

Edd, at aged four, loved anything to do with Space travel and the stars. He was particularly fascinated with the Moon, Mars and astronauts Aldrin and Armstrong. His other interest in science is paleontology.

Using an android slate, the game engine Unity and Qualcomm's Augmented Reality plugin, Vuforia, it was easy to 'resurrect' Dinosaurs. Edd watched in fascination, using the slate as a director's viewfinder as he tracked an animated Triceratops walk around his room.

With the arrival of the Oculus Rift VR devkit, I felt it was time to send Edd on his first field trip, to the planet Mars... Needless to say, he enjoyed "being there" on Mars. He wasn't allowed to wear the headset for long periods as no one yet understood the relationship between the headset's Interaxial separation and a child's interocular. Children have a smaller interocular separation or interpupillary distance than adults.

Back then, studies weren't done on optimal PC config to eliminate other untoward side effects if any, of latency or other potential nausea inducing conditions that might occur in VR in an educational or classroom environment. Headsets do have health and safety documentation that every Storyteller, developer, even school teachers should go through if they are considering introducing VR into classrooms or in home education.

I've only used 2D panoramas of the Moon and Mars from NASA's website, as stereoscopic panoramas would need to take into account the much smaller interocular separation of kids as mentioned, and the stereo pano pairs themselves found on the net were not optimally shot for Stereo comfort. I'd remapped / projected the Panoramas for the headset.

"What if Scenarios" for Immersive Education:
What if...we had all the digital assets of the Pandora world from the movie Avatar, running on a Virtual Reality platform, thus allowing real-time navigation of this fantasy planet? What if... we went one step ahead, and inserted some Artificial Logic, or "rules" into this real time world, as seen in "Serious games" that scientists and environment experts use to model real-world climate change in scientific simulations? Would such Virtual Reality learning, drive home a topic like no classroom lecture ever could?

After watching a movie such as Avatar, it leaves the mind wanting to explore the fantasy world more. It does not become a boring lesson in social morality, but an experience that will leave a lasting impression on the audience, or a study group of young students participating with a teacher in an immersive environment.

Socio-Political lessons via 360 VR movies:
I'm not privy to the screenplay of "The Mission VR," one of the older good 3D 360 VR films by JauntVR. But if the screenplay had scenes for example, from some historic event from World War II, or, if any Hollywood Studio is considering say, an American Civil History film, then, if these fully immersive scenes were made available to classrooms, a history teacher could enable a history lesson, unlike any other! - immersing the entire classroom right onto a battlefield or the aftermath of a civil unrest incident, explaining many aspects that shape the future after the event...far beyond what's capable via a lecture or video.

Virtual Reality - @Home Emergency Learning System:

The 2009 Swine Flu Epidemic threatened to shut down schools in many parts of the World. Countries such as France, had already put in a system in place that would have students "attend" school by listening and viewing lectures via TV Broadcasts and over the internet. Affordable Virtual Reality today allows a true "Parallel World" -a Second Life- type learning environment where students and teachers can attend class, with true first person immersion and collaboration in cases of National emergencies.

VR learning @home, need not be during national emergencies only. For any medical reason if a student cannot attend regular class, there could be an option to don a head-set and log into a secure VR network running on a school's server, so the student could be virtually present in a classroom.

Virtual Field Trips - From the Classroom:

Virtual Reality in the classroom is already here. I remember there being a Govt. Of Australia initiative allowing students to 'raid' caves in VR in photorealistic detail. To put this into perspective...

this is not a game world that students roam around in, but true Digital replicas of Real World locations. The future of Field Trips is here. To further drive the point home about what this means to the future of technology in education, consider this:

- An entire classroom could visit a real world location in their own hometown, or a location half way across the world.

- A teacher could use one single Digital Asset to devise multiple lessons that allows for "revisits." Each student and the teacher could 'interact' with other students' avatars,

- Virtual Reality Exchange student programs: Visiting students can log in and interact with the hosting school.

- Students not able to attend class can log in and still participate in the Field Trip.

❉ ❉ ❉

Moon panoramas are here: Moon Panoramas (https://www.lpi.usra.edu/resources/apollopanoramas/)

Mars panoramas (2D), here: Mars Panoramas (https://mars.nasa.gov/mer/multimedia/panoramas/spirit/)

School kids raid caves in VR: Jenolan Caves VR (https://blog.csiro.au/kids-raid-caves-in-virtual-classroom/)

AFTERWORD

*"...What is it about these electronic dots that
has the power to turn people on?*

*There's nothing real in them, but that's never stopped
millions of people every day, from deriving gratification
by interacting with these points of light...*

It must all be down to our perception of reality..."

— DAN, MEMORIES WITH MAYA.

10 years ago, immersive eye-wear was still hard sci-fi. Now, at least three of the big players in VR are in an arms race to create low-profile Mixed Reality eye-wear. Dan had christened his device a *'Wizer'* (visor+A.I.)

We're not far from that reality, given we have LLMs (large language models) and video see-thru headsets. Besides industrial usage and gaming, XR's higher calling is in human inter-personal relationships & entertainment.

We, storytellers...can help make it happen.

—Best wishes.

ABOUT THE AUTHOR

Clyde Desouza

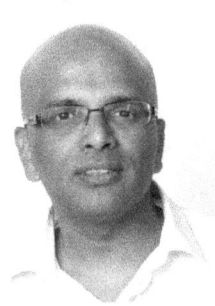

Clyde DeSouza is the author of two books: "Think in 3D", for Directors and 3D Filmmakers. The book is peer reviewed, by Hollywood's top Directors of 3D and late 3D film historian, Ray Zone.

Think in 3D is also part of recommended reading at the Univ of Southern Calif. (USC)'s Immersive Design courses. He is also a published author in the Hard-Scifi genre with Penguin Randomhouse.

BOOKS BY THIS AUTHOR

Think In 3D

After you read this book, you may find yourself critiquing 3D movies more than ever. Stereoscopic 3D films deserve "genre status."

Movies like Avatar and Hugo showed us what's possible... It's your turn now as a film-maker, Screenwriter, Editor or even as a 3D Movie Enthusiast...to take it forward.

Memories With Maya

"EMOTIONS ARE LIKE A VIRUS, a common cold...disrupting the flow of logic in the mind." Daniel reminds himself. Dan's work involves creating commercially viable AR solutions.

He turns to close friend, Krish, a researcher in Artificial Intelligence, in the hope that they can come up with ideas for the Entertainment market. Krish gets a job at the prestigious A.I.R.I. Using AIRI's lab and under guidance from Prof. Kumar; Krish's mentor, they create an advanced visor with Augmented Intelligence built in. They dub it "Wizer".

A Board member at AIRI sees potential in the Wizer other than what Dan and Krish have in mind. At a test in a nightclub, things go wrong...

PRAISE FOR AUTHOR

"Though we're still figuring out what "thinking in 3D" really means in terms of artistic practice, Dsouza is asking many of the right questions about this essential issue." - Ray Zone 3D, Film Historian, Author.

"Got it, Agree with it". - Demetri Portelli - Stereographer - "HUGO" / "47 RONIN."

"There have been many books written about stereoscopic 3D, far more than most people realize. Yet, very few, less than a half dozen, would I recommend as "must reads" for professionals... This book is absolutely among the top half dozen that do qualify.

Anyone who wants to call themselves a stereographer must read this."
-- John Rupkalvis (JR) Stereoscope

"Desouza approaches the subject with a tone and gravity that allows those with an understanding of filmmaking or indeed stereo, easy access, bypassing the mathematical and scientific approach in favour of a more emotional and artistic angle." -- Marcus Alexander, Stereographer, 3D Producer (Wrath of the Titans, Seventh Son)

"It is not so much a "How To" tech manual, as it is a guide to help the reader ponder the aesthetics of 3D in order to better understand how to effectively use it." -- James Mathers, Digital Cinema Society

- THINK IN 3D

In Memories with Maya, human sexuality gets an upgrade... That's what Clyde deSouza explores in his highly entertaining near-future science-fiction novel --i09.com

"He pulls an epic amount of research into his storyline on augmented eyeglass technology and visorwear. -- Ann Reynolds, The Huffington Post.

"If your body died, but you had a mindclone, you would not feel that you personally died, although the body would be missed more sorely than amputees miss their limbs." I think it would be very cool to combine this concept with the advanced augmented-reality technology described in the novel. -- Giulio Prisco, Futurist, Transhumanism editor, Kurzweil AI

In Clyde deSouza's science fiction novel Memories with Maya, however, AI and Augmented Reality add to the transhuman mix (in the form of haptic interfaces) by imagining how we'll interact with the reanimated avatars of our loved ones. The concept is fascinating and imminently credible.-- John Havens, Mashable.

- MEMORIES WITH MAYA

www.ingramcontent.com/pod-product-compliance
Lightning Source LLC
Chambersburg PA
CBHW072209290526
45794CB00004B/1704